POCKET
BOOKS

D0524954

*Also by Dr Bob Rotella*

Golf Is Not a Game of Perfect
Golf Is a Game of Confidence
Putting Out of Your Mind
Life Is Not A Game of Perfect

# THE
# GOLF OF
# YOUR
# DREAMS

# BY DR BOB ROTELLA
## WITH BOB CULLEN

POCKET
BOOKS

LONDON • SYDNEY • NEW YORK • TORONTO

This edition first published by Pocket Books, 2005
An imprint of Simon & Schuster UK Ltd
A Viacom Company

1 3 5 7 9 10 8 6 4 2

Simon & Schuster UK Ltd
Africa House
64–78 Kingsway
London WC2B 6AH


www.simonsays.co.uk

Simon & Schuster Australia
Sydney

A CIP catalogue record for this book is available from
the British Library

ISBN 1-4165-0200-9

Printed and bound in Great Britain by
Bookmarque Ltd, Croydon, Surrey

*To Mom and Dad,*

*for being the best*

# Contents

# INTRODUCTION

Of all the statistics kept by the United States Golf Association, the most sobering are these: Fifteen years ago, the average American male golfer's handicap index was 16.2. The average woman's was 29. As I write this, the average American male golfer's handicap is 16.2. The average woman's is 29.

In those fifteen years, golf has seen the introduction of drivers with big heads fashioned from metals once used for rocket ships. They promised to make the ball go further. Golf has seen the advent of perimeter-weighted, game-improvement irons. They promised to make the ball go straighter. It's seen new putters with long shafts that promised steadiness and plastic-blade inserts that

promised feel. Every week, it seems, golf has seen the introduction of a new longest ball that promised to shatter win-
dows miles from the golf course.

In those fifteen years, computers and videos have come
along to enhance our understanding of the golf swing.
They're available not just to touring pros and their swing
experts; you have to travel pretty far into the country nowadays to find a driving range that doesn't have a video camera
to tape your swing, and a software program that will compare it to Nick Faldo's.

The statistics don't lie: Despite all the billions of dollars
they have spent on new clubs and balls, despite all the
lessons they have taken, American golfers have not, by and
large, gotten any better.


I've played and coached many sports. I got my first taste
of how people learn new skills when I was an undergradu-
ate and taught mentally handicapped children how to swim
and tumble at the Brandon Training School. While in graduate school, I coached high school basketball and college
lacrosse. Since getting my doctorate in sports psychology,
I've spent more than two decades helping football teams,
baseball teams, and basketball teams. I've helped equestrians,
skiers, stock-car drivers, and tennis players.

One thing I've learned is that no other sport would tolerate the stagnant skills that golf tolerates. If a pro-football
owner invested heavily in his team and saw no improve-

ment over fifteen years, he'd fire the coach, get new players, or both. But golf is peculiar. There are no owners insisting on performance. Every player is his own master. Teaching professionals, the coaches of the sport, are often judged more on the basis of how smoothly they run the annual member–guest tournament than on how they improve, or fail to improve, the quality of play at their clubs.

I often speak to groups of PGA teaching pros. When I do, I sometimes ask how many of them know more about the golf swing now than they did at the age of 16. Almost everyone raises his hand. Then I ask how many of them are more confident now than they were at 16 that they can drive a ball down the middle of a tight fairway with a match on the line. Very few raise their hands.

It's symptomatic, I think, of the way that the golf-teaching profession has gotten a bit lost. Somehow, the teaching of the golf swing has supplanted the teaching of golf. It's as if a football coach taught his quarterbacks to throw perfect spirals, but not to pick out receivers, analyze defenses, and pass for touchdowns. The team would lose. The coach would either be fired or he'd change the way he coached his quarterbacks.

If the pro at your course faced similar pressure, if he were paid on the basis of how well your club did in interclub matches, I suspect he would begin to change the way he taught. I suspect he'd do whatever he could to change the approach his members took to lessons and improvement.

If the members' livelihoods depended on how well they played, I suspect they'd welcome the change.

But as it stands, the system in golf is all but designed to evade the truth about improving golf performance.

This book will give you that truth. My previous two books, *Golf Is Not a Game of Perfect* and *Golf Is a Game of Confidence,* covered the mental aspects of the game. This book will tell you what you need to know to develop all facets of the game.

It will not, in and of itself, make you a better golfer. It will not teach you how to swing the driver or how to putt. If you read it on a Friday night, you will not go out to the course on Saturday morning any more capable than you were the previous Saturday.

But reading this book will make you aware of what you have to do to play the golf you've always sensed you were capable of playing.

The fact is that you can't make the journey from average player to scratch player in an armchair. You can't do it by reading books, and you can't do it by watching videos. You can't do it by going to the pro shop and buying new equipment and new balls. You can't do it by spending a few days in a sunny clime at a golf school, nor can you do it simply by spending more time practicing and playing. There are no quick fixes, no secrets.

But you can do it.

The good news about golf is that great physical ability is not required to play well. You don't need the height, weight, or speed specifications they look for in the National Football League. In fact, I'm convinced that the vast majority of the population has the physical talent necessary to play golf at scratch or close to it. I'm not promising that you can become a tour player regardless of your age and ability. I am promising that you can improve dramatically if you're willing to put in intelligent effort, substantial time, and diligent practice. You can start to play a kind of golf that feels simple, effortless, and fun.

In fact, I dare you to follow the program outlined in this book for three years and not make great progress.

What you need, first, is the right attitude. All the great coaches have understood this. They develop players and teams by demanding and nurturing characteristics like desire, patience, and persistence. These characteristics, more than physical talent, enable athletes in any sport to improve their performance.

If you doubt it, look at basketball. The playgrounds and minor leagues are full of guys with springs in their legs and fancy dunk moves. There is only one Michael Jordan. He is very talented, but what sets him apart is his attitude toward improving himself. Michael Jordan is committed to a plan. He lifts weights to improve his strength and avoid injury. He stretches. He watches what he eats. He practices two or three hours a day. And he does these things consistently. He is prepared to do whatever is necessary to keep himself and his game in shape.

Jordan involuntarily proved this in the spring of 1995, when he came back to the NBA after a fling at baseball. It was obvious to all that his skills had deteriorated due to lack of practice. Without the time he needed to hone his game and his body, he was just another player. His raw talent alone couldn't carry the Bulls. But the next season, after he had given himself time to return to his self-improvement plan, he was again invincible.

I see the same principle at work in golf. Nick Faldo has been one of the best players of the past decade. It's not because he is supremely talented. It's because he has spent 12 years with the same teacher, taking the same approach to the golf swing. His intense desire and his commitment to that program have made him great.

The minitours in Florida are full of players who are supremely talented. They can all hit the ball over the fence at the end of the range. What they frequently lack, what separates them from great golfers like Faldo, are the same attributes that separate Michael Jordan from the rest of the NBA: desire, commitment, and persistence.

If you have desire, commitment, and persistence, you have the prerequisites for improved golf. You can be a scratch player or close enough to it that you will have a marvelous time seeing how good you can get.

This book is like a map of the route from New York to Los Angeles. The map doesn't carry you there. It shows you how to direct your own efforts. Similarly, this book shows you the path that leads from average golf to excellence.

Whether you make the journey is up to you.

CHAPTER 1

# The Golf of
# Your Dreams, and
# Why Few Attain It

I have no quarrel with someone who wants to play indifferent golf.

Millions of people want to play a round of golf once or twice a month. They want to enjoy the fresh air, the sunshine, and the company. They don't want to practice or take lessons, and they may have valid reasons. Perhaps young children demand most of their time and energy. Perhaps their careers demand seventy hours a week. They may just not care very much how well they play golf. That's fine, as long as they understand the limitations they place on themselves, and admit they don't want to play as well as they can, at least not now. If this makes them happy, they're welcome to play their way.

This book isn't written for them.

This book is for the golfer who's stopped being indifferent, the golfer who puts or is ready to put a lot of time and energy into the game, the golfer who's puzzled and frustrated that his time and energy don't produce lower scores. It's written for the golfer who is determined to get better, but hasn't figured out how to go about it.

The fact is that improving your golf is more difficult than, say, improving your cycling. Once you've learned to ride a bicycle, your improvement in speed and endurance will correlate more or less directly with the time and effort you put into training. But with golf, time and effort are not sufficient. The quality and intelligence of the effort you put in are more important than the quantity. What I see as I travel around the country playing golf, consulting with players, and holding clinics, is that most amateurs unintentionally undermine the quality of the effort they put into the improvement of their games. They do so in many ways.

Some players have convinced themselves that talent determines who becomes good at golf, and that they don't have that talent. I'm not going to say that talent doesn't exist. I've seen a few players who have never practiced take to the game so naturally that they got to scratch, or very close to it, with little or no effort. On the other end of the spectrum, I've seen a few people who took up the game as adults, having never done anything athletic in their lives. They can improve, but usually slowly and gradually.

These people, though, are the exceptions, a small percent

of the total population. The vast majority of golfers falls in between. They have the talent required to play well. But their talent must be developed properly.

A lot of golfers don't want to know this. It's more comfortable for them to think that lack of talent limits their potential. They spend a lot of time at golf without getting better, but they can blame their mediocre play on God, on their genes—on anything besides themselves.

This is a universal human tendency. I have a friend who does business in Russia. He decided that his work would be more successful if he spoke Russian, so he took Russian language courses and worked with tutors. For several years, he carried index cards in his jacket pocket with Russian words written on one side and the English equivalents on the other. Whenever he had a few minutes, he'd pull out the cards and study them. After a long while and a lot of practice, he learned to speak pretty good Russian.

But when he meets people who discover that he speaks Russian, the most frequent response he hears is, "You must have an ear for languages. I don't. I have a tin ear."

People would rather believe in tin ears than acknowledge that the reason they don't speak Russian is that they didn't put in the hours of study and practice.

The problem with this is that, as the pioneering American psychologist William James realized long ago, people tend to become what they think of themselves. If you're going to get better at golf, at speaking Russian, or at anything else that requires disciplined effort, you must first think of yourself as capable of doing so. You must believe that you have the talent to succeed.

A friend of mine, Robert Willis, recently sent me a videotape of a golfer named Mike Carver playing nine holes on a course in Grenada, Mississippi. Carver shot 35, or even par. The remarkable thing about the tape was not the score, although it was very impressive to see a player being video-taped for the first time sink a 15-foot birdie putt on the last hole to come in at even par.

The remarkable thing was Carver himself. He was born with a right arm that ends just below the bicep. He has only three fingers on his left hand and his left wrist is fused. His right leg ends just above the knee; he wears a prosthesis. His left ankle is fused.

When he plays golf, Mike puts the club in his left hand and addresses the ball with his hand way out in front of the clubhead. He takes the club back with his left arm, rests it briefly on the stump of his right arm, then swings through the ball one-handed. He steps through as he shifts his weight, à la Gary Player. Then he hobbles off and hits it again. He usually hits a nice, controlled draw, and he can produce about two-hundred yards of distance.

His short game enables him to shoot around par. He takes a practice swing, then lets the chip go, and he almost always makes crisp contact. His nickname is Stoney because he so often chips it up stone dead.

At the end of the tape, Mike is seen putting his clubs into

his car, which has the vanity tag "Stoney 2," but no handicapped sticker. Mike, it turns out, doesn't want one. He doesn't see himself as handicapped.

And that's why Mike Carver can play par golf. He reminds me of one of the insights that John Wooden contributed to sport: "Don't let the things you can't do stand in the way of things you can do." Most people, looking at him, would think him not just lacking talent, but severely handicapped. That is not the way Mike sees himself. He thinks he's got talent. He thinks he can be an excellent golfer. And that belief, coupled with patient practice, has made him one.

Without that belief, without faith that you can become an excellent player, you won't have the motivation required to stick with it when progress is slow. And, in learning golf, there will be times when progress is not just slow but nonexistent. There will be times when you seem to be going backwards.

This fact relegates another large group of dedicated golfers to perpetual mediocrity. They may believe they have the talent to improve. They may take a lesson or two with good intentions. But then their pros tell them they must change their grip or their backswing. They feel very uncomfortable with the change at first; quite frequently, they can barely make contact with the ball. But they won't work on the change to make it feel comfortable and natural. They don't accept the fact that this will take time. And they don't let anything deter them from playing their usual tooth-and-toenail two-dollar nassau on Saturday morning.

Along about the twelfth hole, they're five down, they've just hit two poor shots, and another press is looming. Suddenly they're not very enthused about the process of improvement. Maybe they abandon the new grip or the new backswing then and there. Or maybe they stick with it for the rest of the round, fork over their lost bets, and go to the locker room grousing about how the damned pro has ruined their (15-handicap) games. They talk themselves into believing this, they stop taking lessons, and they finish the season just about where they started. The only thing they got from their lessons was, perhaps, a couple of high scores that bumped their handicaps up a few notches and allowed them to win back some of the money they lost. They are too concerned with short-term results to persist in a long-term process.

Yet another group of nonimprovers subscribes to Ben Hogan's maxim that the golf swing is in the ground and a golfer just has to dig it out. They want to teach themselves how to play the game, and they're prepared to hit thousands of practice balls to do it. This is not impossible. It's true that Hogan and some other great players essentially taught themselves. But keep two things in mind: You never heard of all the lousy players who tried Hogan's learning method and found that all they accomplished was to ingrain a bad swing. And, you didn't, if you were a golf fan, hear much about

Hogan until he was in his 30s. He took up the game as a caddie when he was about eleven years old. It took him more than twenty years of constant effort to build a swing that he could rely on.

On the other hand, look at the examples of the other two main contenders for the title of greatest American golfer: Bobby Jones and Jack Nicklaus. Each of them had a teacher who helped him learn the game and remained his mentor well into adulthood—Stewart Maiden in Jones's case and Jack Grout in Nicklaus's. Both Jones and Nicklaus were contending for national championips while still in their teens. Each won a U.S. Open in his early twenties.

So, while I may admire the persistence and dedication of the ball-beating golfers down at the end of the range who are trying to teach themselves the game, I would say that the evidence suggests their method is neither the most effective nor the most reliable. A good teacher will save you time. He'll help pull you out of troughs of discouragement. He'll stop you before you can let mistakes become habits.

Even the best of athletes have realized this. I was recently at East Lake Golf Club in Atlanta, where Bob Jones learned the game. In the locker room, there's a picture of Babe Ruth playing golf. The caption quotes him as saying that to play golf well, you need good coaching.

Babe Ruth epitomized the natural athlete. And even he didn't think he could learn the game by digging it out of the ground.

There is a mistake worse than trying to learn on your

own. I'm thinking of the players who flit from teacher to teacher and tip to tip. These are the golfers who read all the magazines and devoutly watch the swing tips on the golf telecasts. Unfortunately, the backswing tip they see on television probably isn't appropriate for the grip they read about in the magazine, and neither of them may be applicable to their particular swing.

They compound the problem if they go from one pro to another, taking a lesson here and a lesson there. Confronted with a pupil he knows he may see only once, the typical golf pro will try to apply a Band-Aid that will help the golfer get through his next round somewhat less likely to hit a ball out of bounds. He won't—he can't—fix the fundamental problems in one lesson. He feels no responsibility for the way such a pupil plays.

Pretty soon, the golfer who wanders from teacher to teacher has a game that's all Band-Aids, which is to say a game that doesn't hold up. His mind is cluttered with different swing theories. He's the kind of person who can chatter impressively about Pro A's latest article on the one-piece takeaway, about Pro B's follow-through, and Pro C's ideas on the position of the hands through the impact zone. Most likely, he adds to the mix a suggestion from his buddy, Player D, who's never broken 80 in his life. One from Column A, one from Column B, one from Column C, and one from Column D may work out fine in a Chinese restaurant, but it doesn't work in golf. Put a club in this player's hands and he looks like a pretzel maker with fleas in his pants, but he loves to chatter about swing theories.

Then there are players whose mental game, or lack of it, limits their ability to improve. Now, I'm a sport psychologist, and the mental game is what I teach. But I'm not going to tell you that golf is played strictly between the ears. Golf is a game of body and mind. You can't play it unless you can swing the club. You can't play it well unless you have a reasonably consistent, repeating swing; unless you can play wedge shots; unless you can putt. However, the mental game is important. In the upper-handicap ranges, I've seen players go from handicaps of about twenty to handicaps of twelve or thirteen just by improving their mental games. In the lower-handicap ranges, the difference between a scratch player and one who plays to a two or three is very often not a matter of ability to swing the club. It's a matter of recognizing the right shots to hit in certain situations, of picking the right targets, of maintaining composure throughout a round. Those are all aspects of the mental game.

The most common shortcoming in the mental area is a failure to appreciate and develop the short game. If you've read *Golf Is Not a Game of Perfect* or *Golf Is a Game of Confidence,* you already know the facts of life as they pertain to the short game. In brief, they are these: The great majority, perhaps two-thirds, of all shots are played from within one-hundred yards of the hole. No one, not even the best players on tour, has refined the full swing to the point where he averages hitting more than 13 or so of the greens he plays in regulation figures. The scoring payoff for a great putt or a great wedge shot is far greater than the payoff for a great drive. These are not secrets. They've been known for generations, and my books are hardly the only source of this information.

Nevertheless there are legions of players who, if they practice at all, spend far more time practicing drivers and five-irons than they do wedges. If you confront this kind of player with the facts about the importance of the short game, he may well agree. However, he is likely to say that he wants to perfect his full swing before he turns to the short game. This is rather like a college kid who declines to date any of the women on campus because he expects someday to meet and woo Cindy Crawford. He might be praised for setting lofty goals, but he is not likely to have much of a social life.

A golfer who wants to perfect his swing before addressing his short game is trying to turn golf into a game of perfection, which it can never be. He doesn't really like golf as it is—a game of imperfect swings redeemed by good chips, pitches, and putts. He will lie on his deathbed someday, wondering when his swing is finally going to come around.

There's one final category of frustrated hackers—those whose deficient mental games sabotage their efforts on the course. They don't have consistent preshot routines; consequently, they don't hit consistent shots. They can't accept that golf is a game of mistakes, and they regularly lose their composure after hitting a bad shot, turning bogies into double and triple bogies.

If you fall into one of these categories, you should now have an idea of why your golf game has failed to improve. And, if you have reasonable powers of deduction, you've probably already started to understand what's required if you want to play the golf of your dreams.

First, you have to admit to yourself that you want to be good and that you have the talent to play well. Second, you must commit yourself to a process that will, over time, improve your game. You will need patience. You will need perseverance. But you can improve. Maybe you can get to scratch; maybe you'll only get to the respectable single digits. I don't guarantee what your final number will be, and you should stop trying to predict how far your talent will take you. I *can* guarantee that if you fall in love with the process of improvement, you'll find out how good you can get.

I recently played a round with Ivan Lendl, the tennis great, that reminded me of how satisfying the process of improvement can be. Ivan doesn't play competitive tennis any more. He's devoting much of his time to seeing how good he can become at golf. This is a man who's won major championships and millions of dollars. He has all the fame and glory anyone could want, and he has the means to choose whatever he wants to do with his life. He chooses to try to get better at golf. What he learned from tennis and is applying to golf is what's applicable to you:

The satisfaction is in the striving.

If you think about it, you'll realize that getting good at golf is not so different from getting good at anything else that's complex, difficult, and rewarding.

Suppose you're a lawyer, and a good one. You didn't start out that way. You started out, in fact, when you were a child and learned to read and write. Slowly, you assembled the skills a lawyer needs. In high school, perhaps, you were on the debate team and learned to present an oral argument. In college, you picked up research skills and people skills. In law school, you took all those fundamental skills and added specialized legal training. Finally, having passed the bar, you entered a firm and worked under a partner as an associate, observing how he or she conducted business.

Along the way, your confidence in your vision grew. You developed a firm belief that you could be a successful lawyer, which helped see you through all the tedious nights of study.

And, though you did the work yourself, all along the way you had mentors who helped you learn more quickly and more thoroughly than you could have on your own.

Golf is the same way. It helps to have a mentor.

# CHAPTER 2

## PICKING A PRO

How do you find a mentor?

You start as you would if you were looking for a doctor to perform elective surgery. You would not walk into a hospital and ask the first person with a stethoscope to cut you open. You would probably try to gather some intelligence first. Who is reputed to be the best surgeon in the field in which you're interested? Once you had a few surgeons' names, you might try to talk to some of their former patients to see if they were satisfied with the results of their surgeries. You might narrow the list of candidates down to two or three, and go to see each of them, trying to get a feel for their methods, their fees, and their personalities. Then you'd pick one.

You can do some of the same intelligence gathering about golf pros. Who in your area has helped some players along the road you want to travel? If you know someone who started with a handicap close to your present level who has dropped to a handicap you'd like to have, ask that person. Who helped him get where he is now?

You generally don't have to be a member of a particular club to take lessons from the pro at that club. Most pros are permitted to give lessons to nonmembers. Nor do you have to take your lessons from the pro at your own club. If you don't feel the pro at your own course is right for you, don't be embarrassed about it. It's his job to sell himself to you.

All other things being equal, there are benefits to working with someone who teaches at the course or range where you intend to practice. This pro is likely to see you much more often than someone you visit a couple of times a month to take a lesson. Even when you're not taking a formal lesson, he'll see what you're doing on the practice range. He might be able to correct a flaw quickly, before it becomes a habit. It will be easier to arrange playing lessons with him.

But proximity and convenience are not as important as your trust that this is the person who can teach you what you need to know to improve. If it requires a little commuting to find someone in whom you can place such trust, be prepared to do the commuting.

Once you have narrowed your list to two or three pros, talk to each of them. Too many golfers fail to do this. They schedule a lesson instead. They show up at the lesson tee, club in hand. They start talking about swing mechanics without ever getting to know the teacher, or letting the teacher get to know them. The process should be more like the way colleges recruit athletes, with each party sizing the other up and talking things over. Don't feel as if you're the supplicant here. A good pro should be eager to get pupils who want to make the commitment you're prepared to make.

Tell each of the pros you call that you're looking for a teacher who can help you play the kind of golf you want to play. Tell her you're willing to put in the time, effort and energy to do it. See how she responds to that. Remember, you're looking for someone who is comfortable teaching players at your level and bringing them lower. There are some teachers who really don't like to work with average golfers. Ask the pro if this describes her. Ask her what her teaching philosophy is. Ask about her rates. Ask whether she intends to stay in the area or might move on. Ask how frequently she'd be able to see you and how much she'd expect you to practice between lessons. Ask if she believes that a person of your age and ability can get to scratch or whatever your dream is. Ask what she thinks it will take to get there.

Remember that a teacher's expectations can have a major influence on a pupil's performance. This has been demonstrated in studies of elementary-school pupils. Teachers in these studies were told that one-half their class had high IQs and one-half had low IQs. They were given the names of the supposed smart kids and the supposed dullards. In reality, the two groups the teachers were given were selected randomly. Each had some smart kids and some not-so-smart kids. By at the end of the year, the experimental premise had become a self-fulfilling prophecy. The kids the teachers thought had high IQs were doing better than the kids the teachers thought had low IQs. The studies showed that teachers taught differently, and better, when they expected a lot from their students. This is called the Pygmalion Effect.

Golf pros are subject to the Pygmalion Effect, too. A pro who thinks you can get to scratch will teach you the things a scratch player needs to know. He'll take the time to correct fundamental flaws rather than applying Band-Aids. He'll teach you the short-game skills and the course-management skills you'll need. Obviously, no reasonable pro is going to tell you the first time he sees you that he's certain you can become a scratch golfer. He'll need to evaluate your skills, your work habits, and your dedication before he can evaluate your potential. But during your first talk and first couple of lessons, you ought to be assessing the pro's attitude and enthusiasm. If he seems pessimistic, if he conveys a belief that you really can't improve, then you ought to look for another teacher. The process of improvement is a long and difficult one. You'll be more likely to stick with it if you know that your teacher believes you can do it.

You'll notice that I have not suggested that you must go to the most exclusive club in your area, or to a resort where the pro is world famous and charges hundreds of dollars per hour for lessons. Top-flight clubs often have excellent teaching pros. Some of the teaching pros with grand reputations, have in fact earned those reputations and deserve every dollar they charge. But a good pro is where you find him and he's not necessarily expensive.

To take a golf lesson from Gene Hilen, you drive out Highway 60 from the center of Frankfort, Kentucky, pass a couple of roadhouses and a filling station, and turn into a city park called Juniper Hills. You pass a swimming pool and some picnic tables, and park your car by the little brick pro shop. You enter through a glass door with a sign, required by law, that says you can't carry a concealed weapon in a city facility.

Not that concealed weapons are really a problem at Juniper Hills. In all the years Gene Hilen's been the pro there, he's seen only one man pull a gun, and he was not a golfer. He was a fellow from the countryside who was upset because his woman had taken up with someone who was playing in a tournament at Juniper Hills, and he figured if he caught them on the course, he could shoot them both.

Gene handled it. He gave the gunman a version of The Gene Hilen Egomania Treatment—soothing, flattering words that make a man feel confident he can iron out the kinks in his golf swing or, in this case, his love life. Pretty soon, the man gave up the gun and got down on his knees with Gene on the floor of the pro shop and prayed for guidance. In the end, Gene helped effect a reconciliation.

But, normally, all you'll see when you walk through the glass door is a bunch of guys playing nickel-dime card games at a table in the corner, some hats and shirts and clubs and balls on sale, and a friendly lady behind the cash register taking the ten-dollar greens fee, which seems to be a tremendous bargain. Juniper Hills is a wide-open, fairly short, municipal golf course, but the turf is thick and the greens are inverted saucers, just like on a Donald Ross course. When the local pros play in the Governor's Cup that Gene runs there each September, a couple of rounds in the mid-60s are usually good enough to win.

On busy mornings, you might find Gene next to a microphone helping to call players to the first tee. If it's Sunday, he sings "Amazing Grace" a capella just before the first group goes off. Other times, you might hear his amplified voice announcing, "That was the worst shot I ever saw. Take a mulligan."

On a weekday, you're more likely to find Gene on his lesson tee. Juniper Hills has no practice range, but there is a little strip of ground between the first and eighteenth fairways. At the top of it, under a tree, Gene has a couple of patches of Astroturf with a mechanical contraption that feeds balls to the rubber tee. He's 61 years old now, and he doesn't like to bend over to tee balls for his pupils the way he once did. He's got an old truck tire that he uses for an impact bag when he wants to show someone the proper position of the hands when the club hits the ball. But that's about as high tech as Gene gets. There are no video cameras, no computers.

If you take a lesson from Gene, the first thing he might ask you to do is throw a golf ball as though you were skipping a rock on a pond. That's something he learned to associate with golf nearly half a century ago. Gene, the youngest of 14 children, went to work when he was nine years old as a caddie at the Lexington Country Club. He and an older brother used to sleep in the bunkers on hot summer nights, using towels pilfered from the pool area in lieu of sheets and blankets. That way, they'd be certain to be at the club at first light so they could sweep up the caddie yard and shine the clubs, all to impress the pro, a Scot named Alec Baxter. They wanted him to let them carry bags for two rounds instead of just one, for maybe 75 cents or a dollar per bag per round. The Hilen family needed the money.

Gene noticed, when he shagged balls for Alec Baxter on the practice range, that the way a golfer moves his right side when he swings is very similar to the move you make skipping rocks. He was skipping rocks on a pond near one of the greens one day when a rock hit a duck and decapitated it. That was deemed destruction of club property, and Alec Baxter fired Gene Hilen.

When he went home and told his widowed mother what had happened, she was not sympathetic. She cut a switch from a willow tree and flayed his backside. She marched him back to the Lexington Country Club, and confronted Alec

Baxter. "My boy will do whatever it takes to make up for the damage he caused," she said. "But he has to work."

Alec Baxter rehired Gene Hilen.

Gene stayed at Lexington Country club for a number of years, managing to complete high school, get married, and start a family as he rose through the ranks to assistant pro. He got to be a pretty good player, though the closest he ever came to making substantial money from his golf turned out to be a blown opportunity.

It happened when he was playing in a local tournament and had a five-foot putt on the final green to shoot 67. Gene started thinking that Larry Gilbert, who was in the tournament and is now doing pretty well on the Senior Tour, might shoot 68 and force him into a playoff if he didn't make this putt. With those kinds of ideas in his mind, he froze and missed the five-footer. It turned out that his 68 still won the tournament by several shots. The big payday was lost the next day, when Gene went to the racetrack. Gene's racetrack custom was and is to play his last golf score in the daily double, and the daily double combination of six and seven paid $7,200 that day. Gene, of course, had bet six and eight.

He learned something from it, though. He learned that a golfer must stay in the present and not let his mind wander to future things, like what might happen if he misses a putt.

Gene got his first chance to teach when a little nine-hole club in Mt. Sterling, Kentucky, made him the golf pro, course superintendent, and swimming-pool maintenance expert. He still knows a lot about greenskeeping and he could no doubt fix your pool filter if it broke down—but what he really got good at was teaching.

When he was called upon to give lessons, Gene read and reread Ben Hogan's book on the golf swing, and plunged in. Through the years, from Mt. Sterling to Juniper Hills, he studied film of the great golfers from Bobby Jones on. He attended seminars. He picked up bits and pieces about the golf swing from a dozen very knowledgeable sources.

What Gene does when he teaches is try to keep things as simple as possible. He'll spend a lot of time with a pupil trying to get the set-up correct—particularly the stance and weight distribution. He'll work on getting the club back properly. After that, Gene tries not to give his pupils too much to think about. He tells them to fire the right side, just as though they were skipping a rock.

"If you have the coordination to put the ball in the washer and wash it, you have the coordination to play golf," he says. "Although, I've noticed that it's hard to teach bow-legged people."

I first heard about Gene from a friend of mine named Rob McNamara. Rob started learning from Gene as a 13 year old. Rob's grandfather had been a golf pro, and his father was an excellent amateur who belonged to the local country club. When Rob was ready to start playing golf seriously, his father took him to Gene Hilen.

Gene has a way with kids. He usually gets them started at clinics, throwing golf balls and singing and dancing, to get the feel of shifting their weight at the same time as they use their hands. Then, he starts them swinging a golf club. For those who can't afford one, he has a barrel full of old ones at the back of the pro shop.

He teaches them basic etiquette and rules of the game. Then he lets them start in a four-hole league. If they shoot 26 for the four holes three times in succession, they're permitted to move up to a C League, and then a B, and so on. Boys who can break 100 for eighteen holes may play in the Men's Golf Association events.

With boys or girls who show some commitment, Gene becomes a mentor. He has them write letters to him describing what they've learned about golf. He monitors their report cards. He finds little jobs for them to do around the course so they can hang around and play a lot of golf. They clean carts or rake bunkers or pick weeds. "They learn that if you want something free, you have to work for it," he says.

Although it's officially against the rules for anyone who's not taking a lesson to hit off the lesson tee, Gene generally turns his back when one of these kids hits practice balls off the tee, as long as the kid picks them up.

Rob McNamara does not remember taking many formal lessons from Gene, but he had a steady stream of informal ones. "He never said he didn't have time to show me something," Rob recalls. "If I said I was having trouble in the bunkers, he'd walk out to the practice green with me and drop a few balls in the bunker and tell me to go ahead and start hitting them.

"He'd watch and then he might say, 'Okay, Pahds, you're too flat.'" ("Pahds" is a derivative of Partner, and when Gene Hilen calls you that it means he either likes you, or he's giving you the Gene Hilen Egomania Treatment, or both.)

"Feel like you're picking those thumbs up to the sky, Pahds," Gene would continue. "And blast it! Splash that sand!"

Rob would, and his bunker play would improve.

A lot of what Gene did with Rob was directed more at his head. Like most golfers, Rob went through times of near despair. "I used to quit every six days," he recalls now.

The toughest times for him came when he turned 14 and then, four years later, when he turned 18. In each case, age bumped Rob up to a new, tougher level of competition. And for a while, he had a hard time coping with it.

"Gene was always encouraging," Rob remembers. "It was always, 'All right, Pahds, you're still the greatest, it's ridiculous to think of quitting.'

"When things were going good, Gene could be critical of me. But when things were down, he would find something positive for me to feed on. I was so hard on myself. He'd point out where my perception was off."

Gene kept the attention of Rob and young players like him because he knew how to make the game fun for the people who played at Juniper Hills. He might, on a cold day, let them organize a putting game on the floor of the pro shop, starting balls at the back door and trying to roll them some fifty feet, past the shirts and the irons, until they stopped just shy of the wall where the new bags were displayed.

He might, late in the afternoon, let them play "cross-country golf," starting on the first tee, say, and playing to the third green, and then from the fourth tee to a green on the back side. Or he might organize a match in which the best player would have to take on the others using only an old two-iron. If a small plane was coming in to the adjacent Capital City Airport, he'd let everybody rush outside to the lesson tee, whip out their drivers, and try to hit it. (No one ever did.)

This is not to say that there wasn't some serious teaching going on. There was. Over the years, Gene Hilen has started thousands of people in golf, and he's sharpened the games of some of them to a fine edge. Some fifty of his kids have won college-golf scholarships. A dozen have won Kentucky high-school championships. When Rob McNamara was 21, after eight years with Gene, his handicap was plus five—five strokes better than scratch.

What's most important about a pro, then, is not what he charges. It's the joy he takes in helping golfers develop. It's his dedication to the game and his profession. It's what he knows, and his skill in communicating it.

In fact, honest communication is the first essential in a successful mentor–student relationship. Good teachers realize this.

A friend of mine named Hank Johnson, the director of golf at Greystone Golf Club in Birmingham, Alabama, tries to have his first encounter with each new student over a cup of coffee. Knowing that a lot of people might object to paying on an hourly basis for this, Hank usually does it *gratis*. He has a checklist of things he wants to find out about each pupil. It covers the usual data about a person's age and golf background. Generally there's some talk about a particular flaw that has prompted the pupil to seek help—slicing, inconsistency, or whatever. But Hank wants to know more than that. He wants to know the pupil's goals. Does he or she just want to be able to feel comfortable playing an occasional round of customer golf? Does she want to win club championships? Or are the aspirations still higher—regional and national amateur competition or the pro tours? More important, how much time is the student willing to commit to lessons and practice?

With that information in hand, Hank suggests a program to the student. Only when that program is agreed upon do they head to the lesson tee.

This is extremely important. A smart pro realizes that a student will make much better progress if he feels that he's following a plan he helped devise. An old coach's saying applies here: "Plan your work and work your plan."

Other pros and pupils establish communications less formally. A good example of this comes from a young teaching pro I know, Pete Mathews, and one of his best pupils, Paul Buckley. Pete is the head pro at New Orleans Country Club, where Paul is a member.

A few years ago, Pete had just taken the job at New Orleans. He and Paul, whose handicap was in the midteens, were partners in a pro–am in Hattiesburg, Mississippi. After the tournament, they drove home together, and Paul asked Pete what he thought of his game.

It was a critical moment in their relationship. A lot of pros, particularly young ones, would have taken the politic way out and said something polite and evasive. Most pros are acutely aware that if they don't keep the members happy, they can easily wind up selling clubs in a department store. They become masters of diplomacy rather than masters of communication.

Pete, however, did not become a golf pro to act like a diplomat. He wanted to teach golf. And he had correctly sized up Paul Buckley.

"I think your short game stinks," Pete said. In fact, he used a verb that was a little more blunt than "stinks."

Pete knew Paul would not take offense. Paul is a man who likes his news straight. And he had heard worse. He had taken over the New Orleans Hilton in 1986, when it was losing $9 million a year, and turned it into the biggest profit center in the Hilton chain. Then, in the late 1980s, he developed Crohn's disease, a form of inflammatory bowel disease. He nearly died from it. One treatment his doctors ordered was hyperalimentation, in which the patient enters the hospital and spends 36 days being nourished by an intravenous drip. The patient takes no food during this period.

Paul decided to use that time to improve his golf game. Until then, golf had been a casual hobby. But he had a putting strip made of Astroturf, and he bought a book on putting. He spent his 36 days of confinement learning to roll the ball into the hole, an intravenous tube dangling behind him. He left the hospital with a pendulum stroke.

Unfortunately, the treatment was not as effective in helping his Crohn's disease as it was in helping his putting. After another year or two, Paul's doctors recommended an ileostomy, and he had that surgery.

A lot of people would have given up golf at this point. Not Paul Buckley. Like a lot of psychologically hardy people, he looked around for someone to serve as a role model for the life he intended to lead. He hit upon Al Geiberger, who was playing competitively on the Senior Tour after an ileostomy. Paul became a Geiberger fan. He got a copy of the scorecard from Geiberger's legendary 59 in the 1977 Memphis Classic, and had it mounted on one of the walls at the Hilton's sports bar.

That was where Paul was when he met Pete Mathews. He

was playing golf, which was itself an achievement. But he wasn't improving. Paul welcomed Pete's candor. He resolved to do something about his short game.

For a year, Paul took regular short-game lessons from Pete. He practiced nothing but the short game. To fit this into his schedule, he often went to the club at dawn, practiced, and then went to work. His weekend partners couldn't understand why he was suddenly starting to get up and down to beat them. They never saw how much he worked.

Paul's handicap reflected the progress he was making. It went from 14, to 12, and then to single digits. Paul is not an overwhelmingly long hitter, but he gets the ball about 220 or 230 yards off the tee pretty consistently, and he keeps it in play. That and a good game around and on the greens, is all anyone needs to play in the low eighties or the seventies on most courses.

I got a note from Paul a little while ago. He plays each year in an event called the Metairie Seniors Invitational. A few years ago, he was in the fourth flight. This year, he made it to the championship flight. In his first round match he shot 77 and, getting no strokes, beat an opponent with a handicap of five. "It was the most exciting event in my entire sporting life," Paul said.

It shows what someone can do if he refuses to limit himself, makes a sensible plan, and sticks to it. If Pete Mathews had not taken a calculated risk and opened communications, none of that progress might have happened.

Communication, of course, has to flow both ways. The pupil has to feel comfortable talking to the pro. He must be able to tell the pro when he doesn't feel right about something the pro is trying to teach him; maybe the pro needs to find another approach. The pupil must be able to speak up when he doesn't understand a concept the pro is trying to get across. The pro ought to be the sort of person who takes such questions not as a challenge to his authority, but as opportunities for further instruction.

This kind of good communication fails to happen, I suspect, a thousand times a day on lesson tees across America. The pro says something in golf jargon—perhaps about the club being laid off. The pupil thinks laid off means someone has lost his job. He doesn't know how that pertains to a golf club, but he nods gamely, unwilling to admit his ignorance.

And nothing is learned.

I have always felt that if the pupil isn't learning, the teacher isn't teaching. But both the teacher and the pupil need good feedback for learning to take place. I think it's a good idea, near the end of every lesson, for the pro to ask the pupil to recapitulate, in his own words, what the pro has just taught. If the pupil can't do it, then the pro, like Lucy Ricardo, has some "'splainin" to do.

And you will find, I am sure, that good communication is always easier if both the pro and the player have made a commitment.

## CHAPTER 3

# GETTING COMMITTED

I recently met a golfer named Alice Hovde whose story says a lot about the importance of commitment in the process of finding a pro and lowering a handicap.

Alice is a slender, exuberant woman in her early fifties who lives part of the year near the Old Marsh Golf Club in Florida and part of the year in Indiana, where her husband, Boyd, has been state amateur champion.

Alice had never played golf when she married Boyd in 1981. In fact, she didn't know how much the game meant to him until after they were married. And she had no athletic background at all. Her parents had cared nothing for sports. When Alice was in high school, girls were offered a choice between taking gym class or helping out in the school's front office. Alice chose the office.

But she soon figured out that her marriage

would be easier if she learned to play golf at least passably well. It was not just a matter of playing with Boyd. It was a question of being able to engage in conversation with his friends.

"I figured," she says, "that if I took up the game, at least I would understand what they meant when they talked about pitching wedges and five-irons."

So, Alice became a golfer. Her goal was to learn to play well enough not to embarrass herself with her husband. He played in the low seventies. She figured that if she averaged about one more stroke per hole than he took, she would be playing well enough to be decent company.

For a few years, she took lessons and practiced. It was not easy. At first, she could barely get the ball off the ground. She persevered until she could play in the nineties. Once she had reached her goal, she stopped taking lessons, stopped practicing, and stopped improving. She enjoyed the game but, for nearly a decade, her handicap stayed around 20.

Several years ago, a couple of happy coincidences helped nudge her off that plateau. For one, her husband and other people she played with told her that she had the potential to be a better player than she was. For another, Todd Anderson became the head pro at Old Marsh.

Todd is one of the brightest young teachers in golf. When he was a student at the University of Alabama, he got to watch some of the best older teachers conduct schools for *Golf Digest*. He learned from all of them.

As a pro, he developed a quiet, even-tempered teaching

style, and a knack for helping pupils understand what they need to improve, how the improvement should feel, and how they can practice to ingrain a new technique. He drives around Old Marsh in a cart that looks as if he stopped by a garage sale and suffered a bout of low sales resistance. It's full of devices, from mops to lengths of surgical tubing to a video camera, that he uses in the course of his teaching. (Drag a mop across the practice tee and you'll have the feel of the hands leading the clubhead through the hitting area.)

Alice decided to take a lesson from Todd, but she was chary about it. Like a lot of people, she got nervous when a pro asked her to hit a few balls.

On a rational level, this kind of nervousness makes little sense. If your car developed a rattling sound under the hood and you took it to a mechanic, the last thing you'd want would be for the rattling noise to disappear just as he started to check the car. (Which, perhaps, is why it usually does.)

But a golfer who, say, suffers from a slice, is liable to want desperately to hit the ball straight when a pro is watching him. He has the sense that he's being evaluated, and he doesn't want to seem completely hopeless. So Alice's anxiety was understandable.

Then there was the issue of her age; she was 48.

In my experience, no one is too old to learn. Age may make learning harder. But this is usually because people who are older tend to be less receptive to new ideas and new ways of doing things. It's their minds that get inflexible even more than their bodies.

Age may have made them too smart for their own good. They think they know what they can and cannot learn. They put limits on themselves. They sabotage themselves. Then, when they don't improve, they think they've demonstrated how smart they are. The truth is that they fear putting in effort and getting no results.

I'm reminded of Satchell Paige, the great black baseball pitcher. Because of segregation, Paige couldn't pitch in the major leagues until he was past 40. Some people looked on this as a tragedy, but Paige refused to. "Age is a question of mind over matter," he said. "If you don't mind, it don't matter." With that attitude, he helped pitch the Cleveland Indians to the American League pennant in 1948, when he was 42.

A golfer who is middle-aged or older may have to do things that a younger golfer can get away with ignoring. He or she may have to pay more attention to fitness, especially exercises to strengthen the golf muscles and improve flexibility. He or she may have to pay more attention to nutrition. But there is no reason why he or she cannot learn.

The truth is, though, that anyone who puts real effort into an intelligent program will improve. And she will enrich her life finding out just how much.

But Alice wasn't sure about that.

She put up a tough front when she took her first lesson from Todd. She told him that she didn't take lessons well. She told him she didn't intend to practice.

You can imagine the reaction coaches in most sports

would have to this kind of announcement. If the coach were, say Pat Riley of the Miami Heat or Pat Summitt of the University of Tennessee, a basketball player who said he didn't take instruction well and didn't intend to practice would soon be dribbling for another team.

But a golf pro generally doesn't have the same power in the teacher–student relationship that a basketball coach has with his players. He has to keep the members or the customers happy.

So, Todd didn't argue with Alice. Instead, he tried to work on some things that she could improve with minimal practice. At address, Alice had been listing a little to the left. He suggested a more balanced posture. She was gripping the club tighter than he liked, so he advised her to lighten her grip pressure. That was about it. He finished the lesson with a few words of encouragement and told her to have fun. He didn't know if she would be back.

Alice remembers that first lesson as a nerve-wracking experience. She felt as if she were grinding on every swing, but she also picked up Todd's sense that she could improve. She returned for a second lesson, and hit the ball a little better this time. Todd offered her a little more encouragement. He said that if she decided to do so, she could improve. She would have to make a commitment, a commitment to regular lessons and at least some practice.

Alice agreed. And from that moment, their relationship changed.

First of all, Alice felt differently about her lessons.

"I had been so tense. But after we made that agreement, I relaxed, because it was like we were doing something together," she recalls. She started to look forward to her lessons.

Todd's attitude also changed. As a golf teacher in a resort area, he finds it hard to avoid giving sporadic or one-time lessons. If a member calls to say a dear friend is visiting for a week and would like a lesson, Todd tries to be accommodating. The only students he turns away are those whom he knows flit from one teacher to another in search of an instant, magical cure for their golf problems. He tells them he doesn't want to waste their time.

But, what Todd, or any good teacher, really likes is a pupil who's committed to doing the right things for an extended period of time. Alice didn't promise to become a golf zealot, but she did promise to practice a couple of times a week. She and Todd agreed that she would take a weekly lesson provided she had been able to practice. If she hadn't practiced, she would postpone the lesson.

So, Todd's approach to her changed. He started helping her set goals. He figured that before she left for the summer in Indiana, Alice could get her handicap down to 15. She agreed to try. They started working methodically on her swing, trying to improve her turn and quiet her lower body. The improvement started to come quickly. In five months, her handicap indeed dropped from around 20 to 15.

The next season, Todd urged Alice to take a playing lesson. Alice, again, was nervous about it, but she agreed. The playing lesson spotlighted for both of them the shortcomings in her wedge game. As her swing had improved, she found herself more often within wedge distance of the greens on par fours. In such cases, she had tended to try only to put the ball somewhere on the putting surface. Todd told her she needed to play more aggressively, to think about birdies when she had a wedge in her hands. They started to spend more of their lesson and practice time on her short game.

Alice's handicap continued to improve, though more slowly. This is common: It's often relatively easy to knock a few strokes off an average player's game by fixing a big swing flaw that has been causing a few topped shots or shots out of bounds every round. After that, a golfer has to work harder for every saved stroke, and those incremental improvements often occur in the short game. The better you get, the more patient you have to be.

Todd's lessons with Alice by now are not usually concerned with overhauling her swing mechanics. They tend to be about fine tuning—making sure, for example, that her setup with her wedges gets the blade aimed squarely at her target. They frequently go back to fundamentals and make certain Alice is executing them properly. This is common to all sports. NBA practice sessions quite often return to the fundamentals of defense and shooting. Pro-football teams practice blocking and tackling drills that the players have been doing since they were ten years old. Good golfers are always checking things like grip and alignment.

Alice has continued to make progress. When I met her, she and Todd had set new goals for the season. She wanted to get her handicap into single digits, and she wanted to break par for nine holes. I soon heard that she had accomplished the latter, shooting 35 on the back nine at Old Marsh. A few months later, she sent word that she'd gotten her handicap under ten.

Her commitment—to Todd and to a process—was the key factor in Alice's improvement. At some point, any golfer who wants to get better has got to do what she did. She must make a commitment to a teacher. And she must make a commitment to a process of improvement.

A commitment is not a casual thing. I sometimes use the example of a chicken, a pig, and their relative contributions to a bacon-and-eggs breakfast. The chicken is involved in the breakfast. The pig is committed to it.

Sticking to an improvement plan is not easy. If it were, we'd all be slender and shooting in the seventies. It requires a commitment and it requires honoring that commitment. Obviously, you won't want to make a commitment lightly. You may need to take several lessons from a pro before you're certain that he or she is the one to guide you. But, at some point, you have to stop searching and make a decision. The teacher you choose will be your mentor.

This is no different from other sports. I never heard of a basketball coach who allowed uninvited visitors into his practices, visitors who said, "No, let's not play your man-to-man defense. Let's play a match-up zone!" To teach effectively, a coach knows he has to get his players to believe in what he's teaching them and to practice it without distraction.

Similarly, your commitment will require you to shut out other voices. You're going to have to stop paying attention to tips from your playing partners, to teaching segments on television or in golf magazines. If you do see something that grabs your attention and seems pertinent, you're going to talk to your teacher about it before you try to make any changes in your game.

Tom Kite had that sort of relationship with Harvey Penick. Harvey, obviously, couldn't travel on the tour with Tom. And Tom couldn't absolutely shut out the advice that every tour pro gets, largely unsolicited, whenever he steps onto a practice tee. But before he changed anything, Tom ran it past Harvey. He might, for instance tell Harvey that a pretty knowledgable teacher had suggested he needed a slightly bigger hip turn. He'd ask what Harvey thought, and Harvey would listen, think the matter over, and then tell Tom what he thought. Maybe, he would say, that the change could be good for him—but it would mean he'd have to change two other elements in his swing. Or, perhaps he'd say that the change might be good for some people, but not for Tom because of the particular characteristics of Tom's swing. If Tom made the change, it would start changing the character of his misses. Tom made the final decision as to whether to change things, but he respected Harvey's opinion above all others.

That's the kind of commitment I'm talking about.

When you put yourself in the hands of a teacher, you are relying on him to filter all the information and misinformation that is disseminated about the golf swing. He'll be the one to decide what can be helpful to you and how to present it to you.

What you get from this commitment is not just sound instruction, although if you've taken some care in picking your pro, the instruction will be sound. You get a basis for trusting what you've been told. And, if you trust what you're told, if you believe it will work, then you're way ahead of someone who takes the club back with doubts in his mind. In golf, there are so many conflicting opinions tossed about on how to swing, chip, putt, or even hold the club that you have no prayer unless you can focus on one source of advice and trust that source.

Your commitment will also be a commitment of time. Working with a pro will reduce the time you must spend to improve. This book will suggest some ways to compress time, to practice at home, and to get more out of the time you put in, but it will not eliminate the time requirement. To be honest, I have never met anyone who got to scratch by playing on Saturdays and Sundays and practicing for an hour a couple of times a week. I wish I had. Players who get to scratch spend more time than that. They find an hour to practice or play virtually every day. Most people, if they really want to, can find that hour somewhere in their schedules, even if it means getting out to the course for practice at dawn, the way Paul Buckley did, or giving up a favorite TV show or the evening news.

If at present you can't spare that much time, you ought to scale down your expectations until you can. If you can only find three or four days a week to practice or play, you might want to think in terms of getting down to the four to seven handicap range. If you can only find two or three days a week, the best you might be able to do is around ten.

I can't predict exactly how long you'll have to honor this time commitment, except to say that I've never known anyone to get from an average handicap to scratch in much less than two years. It may take you four or six years and, along with the moments of great joy and satisfaction, you will experience plateaus and setbacks along the way.

Commitment to a long-term process will yield one immediate benefit to help you cope with this. It should give you more patience. Because you know you're embarked on a process that you know could take years, you will find it easier to get through days and weeks when you're not only not getting better, you're getting worse.

Great coaches and athletes have this patience. My friend John Calipari has taken over two moribund basketball programs, the University of Massachusetts and the New Jersey Nets of the NBA. In each case, he developed and committed himself to a long-term plan for improvement that he believed in. His plans anticipated that the early years would be rough, but his belief in his plans gave him patience. He built a powerhouse at Massachusetts and I believe he will do the same in New Jersey. I'm not sure exactly when, and neither is John. If you have patience, you continue doing things properly every day and, sooner or later, success comes.

I can't predict when your commitment will give you the golf game of your dreams. But, if you make the commitment, I can guarantee one thing. You'll experience hope and despair, elation and disappointment. You'll test your reserves of patience and persistence. You'll learn a lot about yourself and, in that way, your quest to improve at golf will enhance your life.

CHAPTER 4

# THE HARD PART

If you've read this far, you might well be thinking: *Find a pro, make a commitment, and take lessons, huh? It can't be that simple, that easy.*

You're half right. It is that simple. But it's not that easy.

If it were that easy, golf would not be the game that it is. Everyone would play at or near par. Titanium factories could resume selling sheet metal to the Air Force. The folks who make the latest slice-curing club would have to find honest work. People in search of a real challenge might have to take up something like figuring out the origins of the universe or understanding the tax code.

But golf is a hard game to play well. The hard part, of course, is not finding a pro, making a commitment, taking lessons, practicing, or anything else I've discussed thus far.

The hard part is honoring your commitment. I

learn this over and over again from nearly every successful client I have. One of them is Dan Grider. Dan is an open, amiable man, white-haired and blue-eyed, in his mid-50s. He was born in a small town in Minnesota and he lives now in Sioux Falls, South Dakota. Maybe growing up in the upper midwest, where the winters can seem eternal, taught him perseverance. Maybe the economic vicissitudes of his boyhood, when his father went broke, and the family had to move to a house without plumbing, taught him to handle adversity. I don't know.

I do know that Dan is a man who understands the value of patient effort. When he was younger, he went to work in sales for an industrial corporation, and quickly increased the company's business in his territory. His sales secret was simple. He made at least four calls on a client, listening patiently all the time, before he even tried to close a deal.

Dan's first dream was financial security, and he achieved it in the same slow and painstaking way. He worked hard, saved, and invested his savings in real estate. He branched out into sandwich shops, then into an interest in a casino in Deadwood. (His weekly poker games in Sioux Falls are not for the faint of heart.) Today, it's safe to say that there is no chance he'll ever have to move back into a house without indoor plumbing.

He took the same approach to golf some years ago when he sold his Deadwood casino interest and returned to Sioux Falls. Dan was a pretty good athlete as a boy, and he'd played a fair amount of golf when he was in his thirties and forties.

He had never been better than an eight handicap, and his aspirations were higher than that. First of all, he wanted to beat his buddies at the Minnehaha Country Club. Second, he wanted to make an impact in tournament golf. He had ample time and ample resources. He was ready to work hard at the game.

He turned to Terry Crouch, Minnehaha's head pro, for help. Terry is a second-generation golf pro. His father, Max, was a caddie who rose through the ranks in Omaha to become head pro at the Field Club for many years. Terry started out cleaning clubs, washing carts, and picking up range balls for his father. When he finished college, he joined the PGA by apprenticing under his father.

Max Crouch, like a lot of old caddies, was not much for swing theories. He taught the way a swing should feel. If he were teaching today, you could bet he wouldn't own a video camera. Terry, as a young man, went the other way. He delved into the theoretical aspects of the swing, and he studied under some great teachers: Jack Grout, Bob Toski, and Jimmy Ballard. Over time, he developed a teaching philosophy that tried to blend his father's old approach with some of the newer theories.

When Dan came to him, Terry started giving him occasional lessons. He decided that Dan's fundamental problem was a reverse pivot. For a long time, they worked on getting Dan to make an athletic movement through the hitting area. Dan, as is his wont, listened carefully. His college degree is in engineering, so he could understand and appreciate the mechanics Terry was teaching him. He practiced diligently for a year. He did flexibility exercises and lifted weights. He improved his diet and stopped drinking.

His health improved a lot faster than his handicap. It fell a stroke or two, but that was as low as he could get it. He was frustrated. Worse, he felt embarrassed. He sensed that some of his friendly rivals at the club were snickering behind his back, talking about all the effort he was putting in just to remain their pigeon on Saturday mornings. This is the way, unfortunately, of golf buddies everywhere. They'll always cock an eyebrow at someone who works hard to improve. They'll take covert (and sometimes not covert) satisfaction from seeing their friend fail to improve, since this suggests that their own haphazard approach is not responsible for the state of their own games.

Dan was so discouraged that he went to see Terry, and talked about giving up. "The game is just so hard for me," he said. He was thinking that if he continued to play at all, he'd do it casually, without taking lessons and without practicing so much. He'd just try to have fun and forget about that dream of doing well in tournament play.

Terry reacted as any good coach would react. He bucked Dan up. "You've improved more than your handicap shows," he said. This was true. Dan had begun to develop a swing that gave him a nice, consistent draw, which produced a lot of run on South Dakota's dry summer fairways. Part of his problem was that in trying to improve his swing, he had neglected to work on his short game. He was hitting the ball better, but he wasn't always getting it in the hole in fewer strokes.

Terry suggested that they change their lesson and practice approach to try to make Dan's approach less mechanical. Instead of analyzing Dan's swing and thinking about particular positions he needed to get into, they agreed to try a series of practice drills. These drills, such as hitting the ball with the feet together, or stepping as you swing like a baseball player, were designed to inculcate in Dan a smooth, athletic motion without requiring him to think about it.

Dan had another idea. His girlfriend, Carla Clay, had listened to him talk about his golfing troubles quite a bit. Carla is not a golfer, but she is a horsewoman, and she knew enough from equestrian sports to know the importance of the mind in athletic performance. She had suggested Dan might want to talk to a sports psychologist. So Dan brought that idea up to Terry.

Terry agreed. He knew of me because one of Minnehaha's members is the father of Kris Tschetter, the LPGA pro with whom I had worked. Terry thought I might be able to help Dan get off the plateau he was on. This, again, is one role a player's pro should fill. If the player needs special help, whether it be in psychology, strength and flexibility, diet or whatever, the pro helps him find it.

Terry called and asked if I had time to work with Dan. I asked him to have Dan call me. It took Dan a few weeks to work himself up to placing that call. When he finally did, he told me he wasn't sure that someone who works with tour players would be interested in trying to help a six-handicapper.

"I'll work with anyone who's committed," I told Dan. That was and is my policy. I don't care if a player is trying to break 65 or 95. If he's committed to doing what it takes to reach his goal, I'm happy to help with the mental side of the game. On the other hand, I don't want to waste my time on someone who's looking for a quick headshrinking session that will solve his problems for him.

Dan agreed to meet me in Ft. Worth, where I was working with some players in town for the Colonial. We went to a range and hit some balls. He was clearly nervous, but once he relaxed, he started hitting it well. I could see that he had a swing that was capable of much better results than he'd been getting. I could also sense his passion for finding out how good he could get at golf. I generally don't know when I first meet a client whether the individual is truly committed to improvement or only talks about improving. But, with Dan, I felt a willingness to honor his commitment. By that, I mean that he would give his golf a sufficient priority to attack the problems in his game and solve them. He would be in it for the long haul.

A lot of his problems were in the short-game area. Although Terry had given him instruction on the various chips and pitches a golfer encounters around the greens, Dan had a hard time trusting his skill enough to execute those shots. In particular, Dan had a sand phobia. He had little or no confidence in his ability to get out of a bunker, let alone put the ball close enough to the pin to save par. We talked a lot about the need to start thinking about getting the ball in the hole from around the green and trusting that he had the skills to do that.

It would be nice to report that after talking with me, Dan immediately took his game to another level and kept it there, but it would be inaccurate. Worse, it would be misleading.

Dan went back to Sioux Falls determined to work not only on his mechanics, but on his mental game. He made some incremental progress on his handicap, getting down to the five range. He had a significant competitive success, winning the first flight of the South Dakota Match Play.

But, there were also times when he and Terry would try some new drills to refine his swing and Dan's game would take a temporary step backward. There were times when he couldn't break 80 and times when he thought again of giving up his dreams and just playing weekend golf.

If you want to improve your golf game, you have to accept that this is the way it will be. There will be long periods when your efforts can seem wasted, when your scores don't reflect the effort you're putting in. These will be the times when patience and perseverance will be the most important traits you can have.

Dan and I met again the following winter. He'd made progress in trusting his swing and in his short game. We talked a lot about focusing his mind on the target before every shot, about visualizing the ball going where he wanted it to go.

Still, Dan's progress was uneven. Impatient with the length of the South Dakota winters, he began renting a place in Palm Springs each March for spring training. There, he worked on his drills. He developed a habit I would commend to anyone: He recorded some of his practice results.

He might, for instance, hit ten pitches from twenty yards to a tight pin. He'd record the percentage he got within four feet. The next day, he'd do the drill again and again record the results. Or he might do the compass drill—hitting short putts to a hole from four different directions. He'd record how many he could make in a row. Usually, he would see steady progress in his training diary. If he started the month hitting 60 percent of his shots close, by the end of the month he'd be up in the eighties or even nineties.

This is a variation of something athletes do when they lift weights. Typically, a strength coach has a pupil record his workouts—how much weight, how many sets, and how many repetitions—each time he lifts. If, after a few months, the athlete (as athletes sometimes do) complains that he doesn't see any results on the field and doesn't feel any stronger, the strength coach opens the notebook. Almost invariably, it shows a substantial increase in strength or stamina.

Charting practice drills can serve the same function. If, after several months of effort, you don't see any improve-

ment in your golf scores, you might check the log of practice drills. If you've been diligent, you will no doubt see
some improvement in the number of consecutive putts you
can hole in the compass drill or in the percentage of balls
you get up and down from around the green, or the percentage of drives you hit onto an imaginary fairway on your
practice range. This evidence of improvement can help sus-
tain your morale during difficult times.

And, Dan was having difficult times in the spring of
1996. He was practicing assiduously, doing the drills that
Terry had prescribed, but he wasn't getting better. In fact, he
was getting worse. He couldn't break eighty. His handicap
rose to around seven, about where it had been when he'd
starting working hard on his game five years before.

Then, as they sometimes do in golf, things fell into place.
The timing of this phenomenon can be inexplicable. I can't
tell you why someone's game comes together in a given
week. But the event itself is not inexplicable: It's the result
of hard work.

Dan woke up one morning, went out to the course, and
shot 75. He started to play much better—not always in the
low seventies, but significantly better than he had in
months. He went back to Sioux Falls and, since he had just
turned 55, entered the South Dakota State Seniors championship, a 36-hole event at Lakeview Country Club in
Mitchell.

He played a few practice rounds on the course. He made
a good game plan. He felt prepared. He felt ready to win.

And for the first nine holes, he shot 42.

"I was unsettled on the front nine," he would say later.

Some people would have given up on the tournament then and there, but Dan is a scrapper. He is the kind of golfer who will go into the trees, manufacture a shot, and scramble to save par for the sake of a one-dollar nassau. He was not about to mail in the last 27 holes.

He shot 37 on the back side, then drove home to Sioux Falls and the practice range at Minnehaha. He worked on wedge approach shots. The next morning, he got up, did his calisthenics, and drove back to Mitchell. On the road he listened to the audio tape of *Golf Is a Game of Confidence,* particularly the segment on how Brad Faxon shot 63 in the final round of the PGA to make the Ryder Cup team. He noted how Brad had, even during one of the great rounds of his life, fought with distractions and nerves.

*All I ask,* he thought, *is a chance to be nervous.*

By the time Dan teed off, the wind was blowing, as it often does in South Dakota. It was gusting to 25–30 miles per hour. He reminded himself of the need to relax and not worry about things he could not control, like the wind, or what the other players were doing.

He didn't hit the ball very solidly at number one, and wound up three-putting for a bogey. But Dan's mind was where it had to be that day. He accepted what had happened; he didn't get angry or brood about it. He parred number two and then hit a brilliant three-iron into the wind and within a few feet of the hole on number three. He sank the putt and he was off.

Dan played brilliant golf that day. It was not that he scored brilliantly, though he scored very well. His brilliance lay more in the way he kept himself calm and focused under trying circumstances—trailing in the tournament, fighting the wind. While most of the field got discouraged, Dan got looser and freer with each passing hole, which is the way a golfer ought to feel.

He made double bogey at number 13 and bogey at number 14, when his chipping and putting briefly deserted him. The wind, by now, was howling. Dan hit his drive on the par-five fifteenth into some trees on the left rather than risk being blown into a pond on the right. He punched out, hit a five-iron onto the green and made his par.

The sixteenth hole was a 388-yard dogleg, into the wind, with water on both sides. Dan, feeling the wind blowing at his hair and trousers, fought hard to keep his mind on where he wanted his ball to go, rather than where he was afraid it would. He played the hole perfectly, hitting a five-iron to a spot 25 feet below the hole.

When he reached the green, he noticed that the head pro at Lakeview was talking to one of his playing partners. For a second, Dan wondered whether they were being warned for slow play. That couldn't be it, he decided. They'd had to wait on the last tee. His partner came over to him.

"He wanted to know if anyone in our group was playing

well," Dan's partner said. "I told him you were. He said to hang in there, because all the leaders are falling back. You're right in the middle of it."

"I'm just going to do the same thing I've been doing all day—take it one shot at a time," Dan said.

He two-putted for par, feeling relieved that he had escaped from a hole that could have cost him dearly.

He hit a five-iron at number 17, a 210-yard par three playing downwind. He hit it too solidly. It came down in the middle of the green and rolled to the back fringe, 40 feet from the hole. "This will be the longest putt I'll make today," he said, feeling now comfortable and relaxed. He stroked the putt, heard someone say it was going in, and looked up to see it disappear into the hole.

For a man who had just rolled in a 40-footer after being told he was in contention to win the tournament, Dan remained remarkably calm. His thoughts moved immediately to number 18. He described himself later as "excited but calm," a seemingly oxymoronic state that I think typifies winning golfers under pressure. They know their adrenaline is pumping. They can feel the physical reaction, yet they have the discipline in the midst of all this to stick with their mental and physical routines and execute their shots.

Dan picked out his target on the left side of the rough at number 18, drew back his club—and stopped. He had seen someone's shoe out of the corner of his eye. He asked the person to move, then restarted his routine from the beginning. He hit it well, leaving himself in the middle of the fairway, 140 yards out. He would normally have hit an eight-iron, but he decided that in his nervous condition, he could get it there with a nine-iron. He hit the shot a little heavy, and left himself 15 feet short of the green.

Here, his work on the short game paid off. He told himself to forget about his mechanics, to trust his abilities. He hit the chip to about four feet above the hole. He picked the line for his putt, stroked it, and looked up in time to see it plop into the center of the hole.

Dan turned in a 71. The first day leaders had all struggled in the wind, and he was tied for first at 150. There would be a sudden-death playoff involving four players. He reminded himself that all he had asked for was a chance to be nervous.

He drove into the left rough on the first playoff hole, then played a fine wedge that started right and moved, with the help of the wind, toward the pin. He wound up 10 feet from the hole. He waited for the other three to play. None holed out. Dan's hands were shaking. He thought of how Brad Faxon's hands had tingled on that day at Riviera. He stroked the putt. It was on line. It fell in.

He pumped his fist into the air and tears came to his eyes.

One of the first things Dan did was call Terry Crouch. He didn't get him, so he left a message:

"Terry, this is Dan Grider. Terry—I won! Shot 71! Birdied the first playoff hole! Stayed right with the process, and won! I can't wait to tell you about it. I'm really, really happy. Thanks."

Dan would go on that year to win the senior division of

a world two-man team championship in Scotland. He would make his first hole-in-one, see his handicap drop to three, and be selected the South Dakota Senior Player of the Year.

He would continue to have his down times, too, times when the ball didn't go where he wanted it to, times when it was once again a struggle to break 80.

"You don't ever own golf," he would say. "You just get to borrow it sometimes."

Dan is a great example of what a golfer of any age can accomplish if he masters the hard part—honoring the commitment.

Terry Crouch, of course, is still his coach. He still devises new drills for Dan to use on the practice range. And he has yet to erase that message that Dan left on his answering machine last summer. He takes too much pleasure in listening to it.

CHAPTER 5

# THE IMPROVEMENT CYCLE

You've picked a pro. You've made a commitment. You've vowed to honor it.

Now it's time to sit down with your pro and plan your first 12-week improvement cycle.

An improvement cycle is a three-month program of lessons and practice that can be repeated indefinitely until you are playing the golf you're capable of. It's based on the knowledge of how people learn athletic skills, coupled with the practical aspects of most people's lives. It's designed so that an individual can improve at golf while continuing to make a living and maintain a family life. It is, of necessity, presented in a one-size-fits-all fashion in these pages, but it may be modified to suit individual circumstances.

One key concept behind it came to me first from Davis Love, Jr., father of the touring pro. Davis was a great teacher. He believed that the optimal amount of practice between lessons was somewhere between six and ten hours. Practice less than that, and you probably haven't done enough to ingrain the new skill you've been taught. Practice more than that, and you raise the possibility that you'll lose your way and revert to old habits without your teacher being around to correct you.

If you're committed to practicing an hour a day, and you play once or twice a week, this means that the approximate time between lessons for you will be two weeks. So, in each improvement cycle, you'll take five or six lessons.

As I said, individual circumstances vary. I believe the optimal practice time for most people is about an hour or an hour and a half. Beyond that, they start to lose their concentration and get sloppy. But, if your schedule lends itself to practicing on a different basis—say, three days a week for two hours at a time—don't worry. You'll just have to make an extra effort to assure that you don't slip into the habit of mindlessly beating balls.

The main thing is that you practice between lessons. If something disrupts your schedule and you can't practice, you may find that it's a good idea to let your teacher know and postpone your next lesson until you have done your practicing and are ready for the next step. Some people, though, prefer to go ahead with a scheduled lesson even if they haven't been able to work on their own. Hank Johnson calls this kind of lesson "supervised practice," and it's a lot more expensive than a bucket of range balls. But if you have the means and your teacher doesn't mind, go ahead.

Here, in outline, is what a typical cycle might look like.

### LESSON ONE
Practice i
Practice ii
Practice iii
Practice iv
Play
Play
Practice v
Practice vi
Practice vii
Practice viii
Play
Play

### LESSON TWO
Practice ix
Practice x
Practice xi
Practice xii
Play
Play
Practice xiii
Practice xiv
Practice xv
Practice xvi
Practice xvii

Play

Play

## LESSON THREE

Practice xviii

Practice xix

Practice xx

Practice xxi

Play

Play

Practice xxii

Practice xxiii

Practice xxiv

Practice xxv

Practice xxvi

Play

Play

## LESSON FOUR

Practice xxvii

Practice xxviii

Practice xxix

Practice xxx

Play

Play

Practice xxxi

Practice xxxii

Practice xxxiii

Practice xxxiv

Practice xxxv

Play

Play

LESSON FIVE

Practice xxxvi

Practice xxxvii

Practice xxxviii

Practice xxxix

Play—charted round

Play—charted round

Practice xl

Practice xli

Practice xlii

Practice xliii

Practice xliv

LESSON SIX—PLAYING LESSON

Five days off

There's an extended version of this outline in Appendix A, with room for you to make notes on your lessons and practice sessions and to chart a couple of rounds.

You'll notice several things.

First, I am not going to try to specify what your lessons ought to be about. That's something for you and your teacher to decide.

Early in the process, you'll no doubt want to cover some fundamentals. You need to decide on a grip, a stance, a posture, a ball position, a distance from the ball, an alignment with the target, and equipment that fits you. These are the fundamentals of the setup and you have to learn them, practice them, and periodically check them with your teacher.

The importance of the setup is one reason I advise the touring pros that I work with to avoid scheduling themselves for more than three or four consecutive tournaments. After that much time on the road, their setups usually start to erode. A slight glitch in the setup can lead quickly to major changes, not for the better, in the way the ball flies. So the smart thing for them is to get together with their swing teachers once a month or so to review and check their setups. It will be smart for you as well.

I have no way of prescribing what you and your teacher ought to work on first. That will depend on the flaws in your game and on your teacher's philosophy. Some teachers may see a problem in something fundamental, like your swing plane, and decide to attack it immediately and directly. Others might prefer to work on relatively easier things like your stance and grip before they worry about things that happen behind your back.

Second, you should keep playing rounds of golf during the process. I don't believe in staying off the golf course while you're trying to improve your game. That tends to lead a player to think subconsciously that the goal of the game and the goal of this process is the perfection of his technique. It's not. The goal of the game is to get the ball in the hole in the fewest possible strokes. In the end, your scores and your handicap are the true measure of how well you're doing. To learn to lower them, you have to play.

You'll want to play in what I call the trusting mode. That is, when you're out on the golf course, you do not think about the mechanics you've been working on. You think about getting the ball to your target. You trust that your swing will get it there. Even if your new technique is not yet perfected, you'll have a better chance of executing a shot if you trust your mechanics than if you let your mind wander into the practice mode, where you think about such things as the way your weight is distributed, or the angle of your right wrist, or whether your swing plane is properly upright.

The time to think about mechanics is during lessons and practice. Even then, you must spend a good part of your practice time hitting shots in the trusting mode. The precise percentage will vary. Right after a lesson, you might hit more balls with your mind on mechanics. Just before you play or compete, you'll want to spend most, if not all, of your practice time in the trusting mode.

You'll notice that playing does not count as practicing. Nor does warming up before you play count as practicing. Only practice counts as practice.

During an improvement cycle, you may want to modify the format of the matches in which you play. Avoid bets or tournaments where someone else's success depends on how well you do. If you've got a partner pushing you to play well, you're more likely to abandon the new technique you're working on if it isn't working well at the moment. That may help salvage a nassau, but it won't help your game. Stay away from this pressure. You might ask your friends to play skins games instead of better-ball nassaus.

You should try to make sure that you play in a format that requires you to hole everything and count all strokes. This means avoiding match play, which can breed some habits you don't want. If your five-foot bogey putt can't win or halve the hole, you pick it up. If you're gettting a stroke on a tough par four, you may play for a bogey instead of trying to make par. If you hit your drive out of bounds and your opponent puts his in the fairway, you may mentally concede the hole and play sloppily—remember, you're trying to become a golfer who makes the critical five-footer, who makes par on tough holes, and who knows how to recover from a bad shot.

So compete, but on a stroke-play basis. You can modify your usual two-dollar nassau so that the payoff is for total strokes on the front nine, total strokes on the back, and total for the round. You can press if the gap gets to four strokes.

Start trying to play at least some of the time with golfers who are better than you are. If you're a 15-handicapper and you play consistently with other 15-handicappers, it's going to be more difficult for you to improve than if you play at least some of the time with single-digit handicappers. You want the habits, the techniques, and the expectations of better players to rub off on you.

This has gotten more difficult to arrange, unfortunately, as clubs and courses have become more crowded. It used to be that people would head to the golf course and pick up a game when they got there. They played with a random selection of golfers, including better players.

Nowadays, nearly all public courses and many clubs have gone to a system of reserved tee times. People have to form groups ahead of time, and they tend to play with the same people week after week. Usually, those people are about as good as they are.

So, you'll probably have to take some initiative if you want to play with better golfers. Don't be shy about asking them. I've known enough tour players and top-flight amateurs to be confident that good players generally don't mind playing with average players so long as they keep up the pace and are pleasant company.

Toward the end of every cycle, I suggest that you chart a couple of rounds. This is a way of assessing your game. Like the tests that a teacher periodically gives to schoolchildren, it will help show what you've learned and where your weak spots are.

To chart a round, sit down when you've finished playing and write down every shot you played and the club you used to play it. Then, circle all the shots played with the eight-iron through the putter—the scoring clubs. This will help you get an idea of how important those clubs are. A round I recently charted for a college player I work with, Gilberto Morales of the University of Nevada–Las Vegas, showed 49 of 73 strokes made with the scoring clubs.

Next, take a look at the tee shots you hit with a driver or a three-wood. There should be about 14 of them. If you kept them all in the fairway or on the first cut of rough, those clubs aren't hurting you. On the other hand, if you hit a few out of bounds or into the woods, that's a sign that you and your teacher have work to do on your swing.

Next, go over the putts you made and check every one that you missed inside of five feet. Then go over the chips and pitches you made from within five feet of the green. How many of them did you fail to get up and down? If you find more than one or two in each of these categories, it's a sign that you need to work on your short game.

Gilberto, for instance, lost six shots on short putts and makeable up-and-down chances. They made the difference between shooting 67 and shooting 73. That's an enormous difference at the top competitive levels. If you shoot 67, you're on the leader board if not atop it. You feel good about your game. If you shoot 73, you're back in the pack and people are asking you what's wrong with your game.

I'm not saying that you should never miss a five-footer or

blow an easy up-and-down chance. But I know that when one of the tour players I work with shoots 67, he's not missing many such opportunities, if any. If you aspire to play scratch golf, neither can you.

Some players might not feel comfortable with the idea of a chart. That's all right. The important thing is that periodically you do an honest assessment of your game to find out where you're losing strokes, and that then you work on those weaknesses.

The next thing you'll notice in the model improvement cycle is the requirement that you take at least some time off. It's important to take five days away from golf every three months or so to keep from getting stale, bored, or both. And you can certainly modify the sample schedule to give yourself one or two days per week when you don't touch a club. You want, as much as possible, to look forward to your practice sessions. Time off will help you do this.

If you live in a state with cold winters, the fourth quarter of each year might, of necessity, be spent away from a golf course. This would be a good time for work on your fitness and flexibility. It would also be a good time for working on your swing without a golf ball. We'll discuss that in a later chapter.

I can't prescribe the specific techniques you and your teacher will work on, but I can proscribe an error that pros and their pupils commonly make. You will not improve very much, or very rapidly, if you confine your lessons to the practice tee and the long swing. To play the golf of your dreams, you'll need to take short-game lessons, and you'll need to take playing lessons.

## CHAPTER 6

# A PLAYING LESSON FROM BOB TOSKI

One look at Bob Toski and it's not hard to understand why one of his nicknames is "The Mouse." He's one of the smallest of the great golfers; when he led the PGA Tour in money earnings back in 1954, he weighed about 118 pounds. Jimmy Demaret, who knew that Bob was the eleventh of twelve children, used to kid that "his father ran out of high test before he got to Bob."

Bob has an elfin smile, wispy gray hair that he generally hides under an immaculate white cap, and brown eyes that turn down at the corners and give him, fleetingly, the look of a melancholy priest. That look disappears when he opens his mouth and starts telling stories. He's a great raconteur, full of tales about the days before the PGA Tour was a rich and luxurious enterprise.

He's also a great teacher whose skills have been honed over six decades. Bob has done just about everything in golf instruction that there is to do. He was a founder of the *Golf Digest* schools, and he now has, in partnership with Gary Battersby, his own teaching center near Pompano Beach, Florida.

His teaching roots go back to his boyhood. Bob got his start in golf as a caddie at a nine-hole club in Northampton, Massachusetts, during the Depression. His older brother Jack was an assistant pro there. Bob was deemed too small to be a Class A caddie. As a result, he carried women's bags, either for elderly ladies or for Smith College students. In those days, a candy bar was a good tip, and Bob soon learned that he got more tips when he helped the ladies get around the course in fewer strokes.

So, if he noticed that a woman's left wrist was breaking down as she chipped, he would politely correct her. Even at the age of ten, he had an understanding of the golf swing, a knack for picking out flaws, and a good idea of how to fix them.

His brother Jack taught him both the fundamentals of the swing and the fundamentals of how to teach it. By the time Bob was 16, he was a pretty good player, but, like a lot of small kids, he had learned to play with a very strong grip. It was the only way he could whip the clubhead through the ball and generate decent power. Jack could see, though, that if Bob wanted to go further in golf, he would need a more orthodox grip. The very strong grip would cause him to hit too many low, uncontrolled hooks off the tee.

However, young Bob didn't want to change. He was getting away with the strong grip by hitting his tee shots with a three-wood that had a shallow face and got the ball up in the air quickly. He sensed he would get worse before he got better if he changed his grip.

So, Jack found a way to force him to change. He bought Bob a very flat-faced Wilson driver and laid down an edict. "This is the only club you can practice with." The only practice area available to Bob was the ninth fairway at Northampton. It was right under the window of Jack's pro shop, so Jack could enforce his command.

"But I can't get the ball up in the air with this club," Bob protested.

"That's why you'll have to change your grip," Jack replied.

Bob, with no alternative, took a bag of shag balls and walked out to the practice area. He started trying to hit them with the new club. He hit duck hooks. He hit shanks. He finally broke down, and started to cry in frustration.

He got no sympathy from Jack. "When you're finished crying," Jack said, "you can practice some more and, gradually, you'll change your grip. You're stubborn and you have to learn the hard way."

It took Bob nearly six months of work to master the grip

change. He won almost nothing for an entire summer but, in the end, he had a golf swing that would win at levels much higher than the amateur circuit in western Massachusetts.

He also gained an understanding of some of the problems that confront a golf teacher. A lot of pupils, even when they say they want to improve, refuse to make the changes they need to make because they fear that, in the short run, they'll get worse. So it's not enough for a pro to point out a flaw and demonstrate the correct method. He has to find a way to cajole the student to swing the right way. Bob can't, of course, be as draconian as his brother was with him but, as a teacher, he's devised dozens of little tricks and drills that do the same thing—force a student to break his or her old pattern and do things properly.

"People fear change," Bob says. "You have to shock them to force them to change."

Bob's own golfing development slowed in 1944, when he entered the army. He became an expert rifleman. After his discharge, he turned pro and started winning some local events in Massachusetts. Jack arranged for him to play in an exhibition with three touring pros: Doug Ford, Ted Kroll, and Milan Marusic.

Bob played well that day. "This kid is good enough to play on the tour," Kroll told Jack Toski. So, in 1948, under the wing of Kroll and Marusic, Bob tried the winter tour.

It was not the sort of life that a rookie like Tiger Woods enjoys today. Bob traveled in the back seat of Kroll's Studebaker, nestled behind the clothes rack. They ate at White Castles, where the little hamburgers sold by the dozen in a greasy sack. Bob slept on a cot in rooms where Kroll and Marusic had the beds. Marusic snored all night; Kroll ground his teeth. Bob made $500 that first winter.

"These kids today," Bob says, "don't have a clue what it was like. They want private rooms, private planes. But I wouldn't change it for all the money in the world."

Kroll and Marusic made Bob their protégé. On the tour in those days, there was no money for personal swing teachers. The players helped one another. A lot of the help, Bob discovered, was given not on the practice tee, but on the golf course during practice rounds.

Bob, for instance, used a pitching wedge from bunkers when he first went on tour. Kroll told him, correctly, that he would need to learn to use a sand wedge to cope with the deep, heavy sand they would encounter on some of the courses. He taught Bob how to use the club. Bob remembers getting another lesson, this one from Dutch Harrison, on how to play a dirt explosion shot from a bare lie near the green. There were dozens of other new things to learn.

Bob was getting, in an informal way, playing lessons.

Bob left the tour to become a teacher in the mid-1950s, not long after he won the money title. There wasn't as much money in tournament golf in those days; the players sought recognition and respect, and Bob had earned that. He had a young wife and three small children, and he didn't like being away from home. Of course, he brought what he had learned on the tour to his teaching. He became the best I've ever seen at giving playing lessons.

I heard not long ago about a playing lesson Bob gave to a 12-handicap golfer we'll call Ben. Ben had gone to Bob's teaching center in Florida complaining about his tendency to slice his driver. Bob had, understandably, given him a lesson on driving the ball. Ben had started to hit straighter, longer tee shots—even to draw a few.

The next day, they went to the Palm-Aire Country Club for the playing lesson. Like a lot of south Florida courses, Palm-Aire has an abundance of water but fairly wide fairways. It's not too long, befitting a course where a lot of the golfers are older, but the greens complexes are tricky. The first hole at Palm-Aire is a par five that bends to the left around the shore of a lake.

"The trouble on this hole is all on the left," Bob told Ben. "Set your tee on the left side of the tee box and aim away from the water to increase your margin of error. Our objective in this round is to take no penalty strokes."

He was conveying an elementary principle of course management, one that a lot of players either never learned or have forgotten. Some golfers think it's better never to mention a hazard, lest they introduce a negative thought. In a practice round, though, I think it's best to observe the hazards, talk about them, and pick targets that consciously avoid them. Then, in a competitive round, the golfer can focus solely on the target.

Ben did as he was told and managed to put a three-wood into the fairway. But, still nervous, he hit his next two shots a little fat, catching the turf before the ball, and barely cleared the water with the third, leaving himself a long pitch to the green off wet sand.

Bob, meanwhile, was putting on a display of relaxed golf. He cracked an easy fairway wood for his second shot, aiming right, away from the lake and drawing it gently back into the fairway, leaving himself a short iron to the green. The pin was cut on the right quarter of the green, close to a bunker.

"I'm going to land this about 10 feet left of the pin," he said, and did precisely that. In a good playing lesson, part of what the pro does is set an example. He gives the student a firsthand idea of how an expert plays and thinks.

Ben, though he was taking this in, was still tense in the presence of a professional. He chunked his sand shot and left himself with a short pitch to the green. He shanked that, nearly bouncing it off Bob's kneecap. That left him deep in the bunker, and he couldn't get the ball out. He managed to put the second effort on the green, then sank the putt to save an eight.

Bob said nothing.

Ben pulled his approach to the elevated second green and left himself with a tricky pitch. "You put the ball in a position that cost you—downwind, over a bunker, and blind," Bob said. His own shot had missed the green, but to the right side, which presented a simple, unimpeded chip toward the pin. Bob got up and down. Ben, worried about another shank, barely put the ball on the green, then three-putted. Ben learned something else about course management. Early in a golfer's development, course management skills don't always produce results, because even if the golfer tries to hit smart shots, he can't always do it. Nevertheless, the skills are important to acquire.

Ben plodded along, making a couple of more bogeys with sloppy chips and pitches. He found it difficult to relax. He felt embarrassed, though he shouldn't have. A teacher like Bob Toski doesn't care how well a pupil plays. He only wants to help that pupil improve, and the more of the pupil's flaws he sees, the better.

Slowly, Ben stopped worrying what Bob Toski thought about his golf and started to play the game. He hit a five-iron from under a tree to 15 feet from the pin at number seven. Bob, standing in the fairway, applauded.

"If nothing else, I'll have the memory of Bob Toski applauding one of my shots," Ben said.

"It was a good shot," Bob said. Then he dropped his own approach shot five feet inside Ben's. Bob is still competitive.

They reached the green. Ben missed his birdie putt, pushing it right. Before Bob hit his, Ben asked him what he thought about when he faced birdie putts in competition.

"You want them to break four-and-a-half inches," Bob said, and paused for dramatic effect. "Down."

He holed his birdie putt and smiled as it rattled at the bottom of the cup.

Ben pushed his approach to number eight a little bit and wound up six feet off the green, but still on the collar. Ben's own course has narrow collars, so he asked Bob for advice.

"Putt it," Bob said, perhaps thinking of the chips Ben had chunked earlier in the round. "The objective is to make four."

Ben putted, but he overcompensated for the friction of the fringe and rolled it seven feet past. He missed the par putt coming back.

"It's all right," Bob said. "You're trying to adapt to conditions you haven't played before. Chalk it up to that."

Relaxed now, Ben began playing his normal game of pars and bogeys. At number 14, a 120-yard par three into a breeze, he asked Bob for some help on club selection. "It's between a nine-iron and an eight-iron for me," he said.

"Use the eight-iron," Bob replied. "The front bunker is very deep, but you can putt out of the back bunkers." Again, it was an elementary principle of course management—stay clear of the worst trouble. But it was not a principle that had occurred to Ben. Relieved of concern about club choice, he hit a smooth eight-iron pin high and made his par.

At the next hole, a long par four into the wind, Ben hit his best drive of the day. Then he hit a three-wood that stopped about ten yards short of the green, perhaps 80 feet from the pin. Ben's mind filled with thoughts of the chips he had chunked earlier in the round.

"I'd love to be in your spot needing to get up and down to win a tournament," Bob said. "I'd be licking my chops."

Ben realized at that moment the difference between his thoughts and the thoughts of a great golfer.

He started visualizing the ball going into the hole. He chipped with a pitching wedge and the ball hit the green just where he had intended it. It rolled up, seemed likely to stop, then caught a downslope that gave it enough energy to cover the last 15 feet. The ball broke slightly left as it neared the pin, and stopped a couple of feet away. Ben knocked the putt in for his par.

"Congratulations," Bob said. "That's the toughest hole on the course today."

They hit their drives on number 16, Bob about 40 yards longer than Ben. There was a delay while they waited for the group ahead of them to putt out. They sat in the cart, watching.

"What is it that's kept golf alluring to you for 60 years?" Ben asked Bob.

Bob stepped out of the cart and looked around. "It gives me peace of mind like nothing else," he said. "It's got beauty, sunshine, and fresh air. And it's challenging. Each hole is different. I don't need a lot of people cheering. I just need to be out here figuring out how to play each shot."

He stepped up to his ball with a five-iron and hit a low line drive that never got more than ten feet off the ground. It landed ten yards in front of the green, took one big hop, then rolled gently up onto the green and stopped hole high.

"That's a lost art, that shot," Bob said, pleased with himself. "It's not taught anymore. Now it's all hit it high, bomb the green, and sink the putt. But I like the artistry of the game. There are so many shots you can play. It's like playing all the instruments in a 14-piece orchestra. If you recorded them all separately and then blended the recordings, people would say, 'That's great music. Who's in the orchestra?' And I'd tell them, 'Bob Toski plays every instrument.'"

He laughed.

They finished numbers 16 and 17 with a par and a bogey and a bogey and a par. Ben had learned a lot about the way a pro manages his game and how he thinks. He had seen a little bit of the shot repertoire of a great golfer. He had learned something about his own swing flaws. He asked Bob what he ought to be concentrating on in his next five lessons.

"Short game, bunker game, putting," Bob said.

Ben nodded, thinking that he still wanted to work on his slice. And the next two lessons?

"Short game, bunker game, putting," Bob repeated. "Your short game doesn't hold up under pressure."

Thinking back, Ben had to agree.

• • •

The last exchange between Bob and Ben suggests one of the biggest benefits of the playing lesson. It's not just what it teaches the pupil. It's what it teaches the pro about the pupil. The playing lesson is a great diagnostic tool. It shows the pro what his pupil's game is really like. It shows both of them where they ought to focus during upcoming lessons. In fact, Bob Toski has told me that if he could start his teaching center over again, he would try to get enough land to build three or four practice holes around its perimeter, just for playing lessons.

Yet, most pros and most golfers rarely give or take playing lessons. Imagine a basketball coach who drilled his team during the week and then went fishing on game day. How could he know his team's strengths and weaknesses if he didn't watch it in competition? How could he convey the nuances of strategy if he wasn't there? He couldn't. He would be employed about as long as a member of the Flat Earth Society would last at NASA.

Pros and pupils have given me various reasons why the playing lesson is as rare these days as a persimmon driver. Courses are crowded. Playing lessons take longer; a busy teacher can't see as many pupils. They cost more.

All of those things are true, but they don't justify leaving playing lessons out of any intelligent plan of improvement. Serious pupils and serious teachers find the time for them. They go off early in the morning, on the back side of their course, or they do it in the twilight hours of summer. A playing lesson need not be 18 holes. Six or nine holes is long enough, but you need to take one every few months, as indicated in the outline of the improvement cycle.

At first, your playing lessons will be disproportionately diagnostic. They will give your teacher a chance to familiarize himself with the real strengths and weaknesses of your game—which may not be the ones you perceive. They'll give you both something to go on as you plan the lessons you'll be taking in the next improvement cycle. That's why I recommend taking one early on in your relationship with your teacher, and then at the end of each improvement cycle thereafter.

As time goes by, the character of your playing lessons will change. They'll start to focus more on special situations you may encounter in a round of golf—hilly lies, thick rough, and so on. They'll help the pro deal with things like your preshot routine. They'll focus more on analysis and strategy—the essence of course management. Above all, they'll help you to learn the myriad of skills you'll need if you want to have the short game of a scratch player.

## CHAPTER 7

# ONE STROKE AT A TIME

A Florida golfer named Patty Pilz knows a great deal about how playing lessons can help develop the short game, and how important the short game is. That's partly because the short game almost caused her to give up golf.

When Patty was a little girl, she played a lot of golf with her father, who was a scratch player. They owned a big half-vacant lot, and her father used to mow some rudimentary greens and tees into the grass there. On long summer evenings, she'd go out with her father and bang balls around. She was an all-around athlete, involved in swimming and tennis as well as golf, and she got to be pretty good. In fact, she was far and away the best player entered in the girls' junior championship at Brookside Country Club the summer she was 12 years old.

Patty was cruising in that nine-hole, stroke-play event when she got to number eight, an uphill par four. She hit her approach shot into a deep sand bunker to the right of the green.

And she couldn't get it out.

She took her wedge and tried to explode the ball up over the lip.

Whump.

It hit the bank in front of her and rolled slowly back to her feet. She tried again. Whump. Same result. She tried again, and again, and again. It didn't occur to her to chip out backwards and play to the green from a grass lie. She flailed at the ball until finally, she managed to lift it over the lip and onto the green.

It had taken her 12 strokes to get out. She lost the tournament, and the trophy, by a stroke.

Traumatized, Patty played no competitive golf for ten years. She stuck to tennis, and she was good enough at it to get a college scholarship. But, in her senior year, because she had transferred from one college to another, her tennis eligibility was gone. She decided to give golf another try and made her college team. Within a year or so, just by dint of playing more, she got her handicap down to about 13.

She kept playing after college. She resettled in Florida, where her parents had retired. Some eight years ago, her handicap was about ten. She heard from a friend about a pro named Bill Davis at the Jupiter Hills Club, which her parents belonged to. For Christmas, she asked them to give her some lessons from him.

Bill Davis, as it happens, is one of the great short-game teachers. He works with touring pros, including Jerry Kelly, a client of mine. He works, of course, with the members of his club. And he takes on a limited number of pupils from outside the club. These nonmembers are some of his best pupils, because Bill doesn't have to accept them. He works only with those who are willing to follow his ideas about the right way to improve their golf games.

When people call about lessons from outside the club, Bill has long conversations with them on the telephone. He finds out how long they've been playing golf, how often they practice, how often they've taken lessons, what their goals are.

Then, if he likes what he hears, he offers them a deal. He will give them them ten lessons, but they must pay for all ten in advance. They must practice between lessons, following a practice plan he will draw up for them. If, after ten lessons and the concommitant practice, they have not improved, he will refund their money.

No one, Bill says, has ever asked for the refund.

That's partly because, very early on in this process, Bill emphasizes the short game.

Not enough pros and players do this, in my opinion. That's partly because of the nature of most pro–pupil relationships. The pupil typically controls the lesson agenda because he comes for one lesson at a time, and with a specific complaint. If he says, "I want help adding distance to my tee shots," the pro generally doesn't feel he can say, "No, let's have a lesson on chipping."

This, I suspect, will be increasingly true now that Tiger Woods has arrived on the scene. Tiger is going to persuade a lot of people, including tour pros, that distance is the key to success. They are going to ask their teachers to help them add distance. There's no doubt that the person who can hit the ball three hundred yards and keep it in the fairway has an advantage over the person who hits it two hundred and fifty yards.

But it's not a decisive advantage. Don't forget that Tiger Woods came to Augusta at the age of 19 hitting the ball every bit as far as he did when he won the Masters at the age of 21. The difference between 1995 and 1997 was that Tiger had polished his scoring game. He hit his short irons and wedges precise distances. He putted better. His course management was smarter.

Many great players learned the short game first and then polished the long game. In an earlier era, they were caddies who spent their spare time playing chipping and putting games with the other caddies for pocket change. Nowadays, I see players like Jose Maria Olazabal and Phil Mickelson, who polished their shorts games early because they had backyard greens or, in Olazabal's case, lived on a golf course where his father was superintendent.

Most team sports have an analogous dichotomy between flashy skills that are fun to practice and subtler skills that a lot of athletes don't want to work on. This problem is solved by giving authority to a coach or manager. A baseball team can't come to spring training and decide to spend all of its time playing home-run derby in batting practice against fat, three-quarter speed pitches. The manager, if he knows what he's doing, is going to insist that the team spend many hours working on throwing to the right cutoff men, sacrifice bunts, and hitting behind runners. Those are the little skills that win baseball games.

A basketball coach, if he knows what he's doing, will not let his team spend all its practice time on run-and-gun scrimmages. He will insist that every day the team work on defense, rebounding, and free throws. He knows that a team will have nights when its shooting is off, when all of the players lay bricks. Good teams win on those nights because they always play defense, always rebound, and always hit a high percentage of their free throws.

Most golf pros don't teach the short game enough because they don't have the authority of a baseball manager or a basketball coach. But Bill Davis, with his outside pupils, has that authority. Once they've paid for ten lessons, they are in his hands. He devises the curriculum. And he makes sure it includes lots of short-game lessons.

This leads to a certain irony. The nonmembers who take lessons from Bill at Jupiter Hills are on a more certain path to improvement than the members who pick and choose what they want Bill to teach them. That's the way golf is. Most people don't choose to learn the short game.

Once he gets a player into his program, Bill is not quick to teach putting mechanics. He believes that touch, a feel for distance, is what most average players need to learn first on the greens. To help them develop it, he has a number of practice drills. In one of them, he has players stroke putts to a hole with a club shaft set down on the grass an inch or so behind it, perpendicular to the line of the putt. They win an imaginary dollar for every putt that goes in the hole or winds up resting against the shaft. But they lose three dollars for every ball that runs over the shaft. They lose fifty dollars for every shot that doesn't either touch the shaft or go in the hole. Bill tells them that after they've won a few hundred imaginary dollars in this touch drill, they can have a lesson in putting mechanics if they still want it.

Of course, not many players do. If they've worked on their sense of pace enough to earn lots of imaginary dollars in his touch drill, they're generally delighted with how much their putting has improved.

This drill is not the only one that can improve touch. Nor will all pros decide to work on touch first. Others may want to fix a player's putting mechanics right away. It depends on the player and the teacher. The most important thing is that the pro and pupil agree on a putting-improvement program that the player makes part of his practice routine from the outset.

To teach other facets of the short game, Bill likes to take his pupils out on the golf course for a slightly different type of playing lesson than the one Bob Toski gave in the last chapter. He gets in a cart with them, and they drive from one potential playing situation to another. Not long ago, he gave this kind of lesson to Patty.

They stopped near a green and he dropped some balls about twenty-five feet from the putting surface, at a spot where players departing the green had matted down the rough with their feet. Bill dropped his hat on the green to simulate a tight pin.

"What's the best way to get to this pin?"

"Putter," Patty said. It was a creative answer, and Bill felt it was the correct answer. The lie was tight, and the footsteps had matted the grass and made it possible to roll the ball through the rough. Using a wedge from that spot, Patty felt, would have brought into play the possibility of chunking it or skulling it.

Other players and teachers might feel a different shot was best in that situation. It would depend on their skills and the condition of the greens they play. But saving strokes from odd spots around the green is frequently what enables a player to pare those last few strokes off her handicap. The important thing is not so much what type of shot you choose to play. The important thing is that, whatever the situation, you have a shot that you've practiced and that you feel you can put in the hole.

Bill stopped at another hole about 40 yards from the green and dropped a few balls into heavy rough. To make sure the lie was bad, he tamped them down with his feet.

"Put one on the green," he challenged.

Patty looked at the green and the two bunkers lying beyond it. She swung—and lofted the ball short. It plopped down in the fairway about five yards in front of the green.

Then she swung harder, and the ball floated out and onto the putting surface. "When the ball's deep in this Bermuda rough, the grass is going to slow the clubhead down," Bill explained. "But most people forget that when they see the bunkers behind the green. They don't hit it hard enough."

He dropped some more balls, much closer to the green but, again, deep in the heavy rough. He showed Patty a "pillow shot," which she could play in such situations, treating the rough like sand and exploding the ball out.

Then, he dropped a couple of balls in the fairway about 20 yards short of the slightly elevated green. He showed Patty a bump-and-run shot she could play if she didn't want to hit a lob off the tight lie. Bill believes that getting the ball on the ground and rolling it is often a wiser choice around the greens than flying it to the pin.

And that is what his on-the-course short-game lessons are largely about—recognizing situations and picking the smartest shot. This is one of the abilities that distinguishes a player with a handicap of six from a player with a scratch handicap. There may not be much to choose from in the two players' long games. Both can hit the ball pretty well and both might hit, say, eight, ten or 12 greens per round.

It's on the holes where they don't hit the greens that the scratch player often separates himself from the six-handicapper. The scratch player is usually better at recognizing different situations, choosing the smartest shot to play, and executing it.

Bill extended this kind of teaching to the green and back into the fairway as he and Patty rambled about the course, looking for gaps between groups playing regular rounds. They stopped in the fairway of one hole and dropped some balls about 150 yards from the center of the green on a downhill lie. The wind from the nearby ocean was blowing stiffly into Patty's face. What, Bill asked, was the right shot to play?

Patty, as it happened, didn't have an iron she could hit into the wind far enough to carry the yawning bunker in front of the green. She hits the ball solidly and consistently, but not particularly long. She could reach the green with a fairway wood. If she did, Bill pointed out, her ball wasn't likely to stop on the shallow putting surface. It would most likely wind up in one of the back bunkers, leaving her with a treacherous shot back.

In this situation, he told her, the smart play was to aim away from the green. Her target would be the fairway area just in front and to the right of the green. Aiming there would take both the front and rear bunkers out of play, and it would give her a reasonably easy chip to the pin and a better chance to make par than she'd have from either of the bunkers.

This wouldn't be the right play for everyone. Longer hitters, obviously, might be able to get an iron high enough into the air to clear the front bunker and still hold the green.

On days when the wind was blowing from another direction, it might not be the right play for Patty, but on this particular day, from this particular spot, it was.

On another hole, Bill dropped some balls in the fairway about 150 yards from an L-shaped green with the pin tucked in the back right quadrant, protected by a large bunker. He asked Patty to pick a target. Correctly, she chose the left side of the green. She would have a long birdie putt if she hit it there, but she was still more likely to make par than she would be if she went for the pin and missed. Again, this kind of judgment is one of the things that separates good golfers from excellent golfers.

In the beginning, of course, not all of Patty's lessons went this way. She came to Bill with a weak, high fade as her characteristic shot.

"She didn't have much motion," Bill recalls. "She could have swung in a phone booth."

Though they worked from the inception on the short game and course management, they initially spent a greater proportion of their time on the long game than they do now. Bill wanted Patty to hit with a lower trajectory. It was not easy, but she came out of the process with a more powerful, consistent shot.

She also came out with what golfers call a predictable miss. In Patty's case, it is to the right. If she mishits a shot, it might fade more than she'd like, but it will not go to the left.

Most scratch players have something similar. They want to know that if they step on to the tee of the toughest hole on a given golf course, with a match or a tournament on the line, they can play the hole knowing that whatever else might happen, they are not going to miss in one direction or the other. Some players know they're not going left. Jack Nicklaus, Ben Hogan in his prime, and Bruce Lietzke are good examples. Arnold Palmer and Brad Faxon, on the other hand, know they're going to hit draws in most tight situations. It helps with planning a strategy. It helps with confidence. Once Patty had a predictable miss, she could make the kinds of judgments Bill was asking for. She could aim for the left side of a green knowing that she would not miss on the left side.

Their work on the swing gave Patty something else to make her more consistent, something she and Bill call medicine. Bill and Patty know that with her swing, the most common problem she will have on the golf course is blocking the ball to the right, because she doesn't properly shift her weight through the hitting zone. When this happens now, though, Patty has a way to recapture the feel of the right movements. She stands off away from the ball, a club in her hands, and makes a couple of baseball swings. Then, with the right feel restored, she begins her normal preshot routine and swings without thinking of mechanics.

This is the best way to handle mechanical problems during a round of golf. You will only know the proper drill to restore feel if you work one out with a pro who knows your swing and its tendencies.

Of course, Patty's progress only looks smooth and easy in

retrospect. Like any improving player, she suffered her share of reversals. She can remember times, playing in club tournaments, when her new mechanics were so awkward that she could barely get the ball off the tee. This is one of the testing moments awaiting most golfers who try to improve.

Her friends and playing partners, she recalls, would quietly suggest that she do things that amounted to going back to her old way of swinging. This is, again, the feedback a lot of golfers get from their friends. There is a strong, perhaps unconscious, urge on the part of most golfers to see everyone they play with conform to a norm. When they see someone trying to rise above the norm, it makes them uncomfortable. At the first opportunity, they're liable to make suggestions that amount to giving up and going back to the old way of doing things.

Patty responded to this kind of peer pressure with an inner strength. She learned to smile, nod, and continue to do what Bill had taught her. She had faith that in the long run, it would work. She honored the commitment she had made.

It took a while, because Patty was holding down a job as she went through this process. She could not practice every day. She practiced on her days off. When she played golf, she tried to go out in informal situations where she could sometimes hit two or three shots from the same spot and work on what she was learning.

Then, suddenly, her game came around and she had the pleasure of hearing the Doubting Thomases reverse themselves. Instead of suggesting that she swing the way she once had, they were asking where she had learned to hit the impressive shots she was hitting.

As her swing and game became more fundamentally sound and her handicap dropped, the nature of Bill and Patty's relationship evolved. She took lessons less often. When she did, she spent less time working on her swing and more time on her short game and on her mental game. This is a natural progression.

It took Patty six years of effort, but she finally reached scratch a year or so ago.

"What winds up happening in going from nine to scratch," she says, "is that you do things in ones. You start taking one fewer putt per round. You start getting up and down one more time. You pick out a better target once per round. And gradually, you get there."

In the past few years, she's won her club championship and played twice in the U.S. Mid-Amateur. Bill has helped her banish whatever lingering doubts there were from that disastrous tournament round at Brookside Country Club when she was 12 years old.

Last year, Patty was playing in a major women's amateur event in south Florida, the Tri-County. She had the lead going into the final round, but she was nervous, afraid she would blow it in the final holes, just as she had as a youngster.

"I'll make you a bet," Bill said. "The stakes are one dollar times the number of the hole you're playing. If you par the hole, no blood. If you birdie it, you win a dollar times the number. If you make bogey, you lose a dollar times the number of the hole."

Patty took the bet. The next day, she didn't think too much about where she stood in the tournament; she thought about her bet with Bill. As she came down the stretch, she only wanted to make sure she didn't lose money to her coach.

Bill got a call that night. "Sit down," Patty said. "You owe me five-seven dollars."

"Great," Bill said.

"And, by the way," Patty continued. "I shot seventy-six and won the tournament by six strokes."

Bill paid off that night, throwing in a bottle of champagne. Patty still has the $57 in a scrapbook. That's the kind of joy and satisfaction that can come to both sides of the pro-player relationship.

# CHAPTER 8

# THE PSYCHOLOGY OF A
# SWING CHANGE

A major swing change is a little like surgery. I don't know too many people who would elect to go under the knife before they'd tried other, less drastic, alternatives for getting better—medicine, diet, physical therapy, fitness. In much the same way, I think players and teachers should, in most cases, look for the simplest and least drastic ways to get better.

This certainly means that they'll go to work on the player's short game from the outset of the player's improvement program. It usually means that they'll wring whatever improved scoring they can out of enhanced basics like grip, posture, and alignment. It will often mean that the pro will look for shortcomings in the player's strength and flexibility. If she's not an expert in those areas, she'll send the player to someone who is. Many swing flaws are actually due to stiffness or weakness in some part of the anatomy. A lot of golfers can improve by getting stronger and more flexible.

It certainly means that a player and his pro will want to assess the player's mental game. Does he have a consistent, sound preshot routine? Does she pick out small targets and think about getting the ball to them? Does he trust his swing when he plays? No one has a perfect swing. No one needs a perfect swing. There are many golfers playing at scratch or better despite flawed swings because they trust the mechanics they have.

But, in some cases, after all of these questions have been addressed, the pro and player will decide that a swing change is necessary.

They should not embark on a swing change without discussing it thoroughly.

First of all, is the change appropriate? If the player is, for instance, a tournament player, will the new ball flight that can be expected from the change be effective on the courses he has to play?

Second, how does the pupil learn best? Some players are analytical thinkers. They respond best to a long discussion of the new techniques and why they work. Others are visual learners who might respond best to a video that shows their current swing and how it deviates from the better swing the pro wants to teach them. Others might be "feel" learners who want to know how the new movements are supposed to feel. Most of us are a combination of all three, weighted in one direction or another. We all want to get to the stage where we are feel golfers, who perform the right movements without thinking about them, because they feel right.

This discussion ought to encompass two more points. One is how long the pro thinks the player will need to make the proposed change. Two is whether the player is prepared for the possibility of getting worse before getting better. This is very likely, because any fundamentally new movement will feel awkward for a while.

Good communication about these pitfalls will make the swing change a little bit like wading across an unknown river in the daylight, as opposed to wading across in pitch darkness. In the daylight, the wader can see the bank on the other side. Even if the water starts rising, he strides ahead. If it rises over his head, he's prepared to swim for a while because he can see that bank and knows roughly how long it will take to get there. The wader who starts out in darkness is likely to panic if the water gets high, because he doesn't know where he's going. He'll turn back or, worse, thrash around and drown.

So, you ought to have a plan and, if possible, a model. It's helpful if the teacher can show the pupil pictures or film of a touring pro who makes the move the pupil needs to master. That's like having the bank on the other side of the river to look at.

As you embark on a swing change, it's important to know that two of the chief challenges you face are habit and comfort.

Most golfers have a dominant habit or tendency. This is a deeply ingrained physical pattern that probably has its roots in childhood. Bob Toski, for instance, thinks that most right-handed golfers tend to slice the ball because they began in infancy to reach for things with their right hand, and reaching with the right hand is not a sound way to commence a downswing. He may be right. Or, it may be that most golfers start out without instruction and develop bad habits unconsciously and haphazardly. I don't know and it's not important unless you're trying to develop a golfer from infancy.

The fact is that dominant habits exist, and they will show up. Each time you swing, your dominant habit is trying to assert itself. This is especially true under pressure. You need good, sound, dominant habits.

So, you must find a way to break the dominant habit you have, assuming it's one that is impeding your golf swing. You must replace it with the correct habit. This can be a long process, longer than the process of developing a new habit where none existed before.

In general, people learning new sports skills or breaking old habits go through three stages. In the beginning, they are unconsciously incompetent: That is, they're doing it wrong, but they're not aware of it. After instruction, they pass through a long intermediate stage, where they are consciously competent. This means that they know the right movement and can execute it, but only if they think about it and direct their body with their conscious mind. Finally, they reach the advanced stage of unconscious competence. In golf, this means that a player swings correctly without thinking about it. In other words, his dominant habit has become a correct habit. It will show up under stress. He can focus on his target with trust that his body will perform properly. And his body, in most cases, will do what he wants it to. Until you reach this automatic stage, you haven't really learned your new move.

Comfort is the enemy of this process.

No matter how bad a person's swing might be, it usually feels pretty good to that individual. He's done it thousands of times. He's used to it. He just can't understand why this comfortable motion keeps producing bad shots.

Take, for instance, a player with a problem on short pitches from tight lies. Sometimes he chunks them. Sometimes he blades them. He's reached the point where he doesn't trust his wedge, which exacerbates his problem. He goes to a pro for help.

The pro might see that the player has two bad habits. He takes the club back too far inside the proper plane of the swing, and he's got too much lower body motion.

The player may have a hard time believing what the pro is saying to him. It doesn't feel to him as if he's taking the club back inside. It doesn't feel to him as if he's moving too much from the hips down. In fact, he feels quite graceful. Of course, he can't see where the club goes once it leaves his field of vision, which is centered on the ball. He can't see what his legs are doing.

Even if he trusts his pro, or the pro shows him his movements on videotape, it will not be easy for him to change. That's because human beings are not objective judges of their own motions. If the player in question changes his backswing path so that the club moves just half an inch further to the outside, it will feel to him as if it's moved a foot. If he quiets his legs just a little bit, it will feel to him as if he's swinging with stiff, locked knees. To make the new, correct motion, a player will most likely have to feel as if he's exaggerating the movement. If he's trying to nudge his swing path a few inches to the outside, he'll have to feel as if he's pushing the club out somewhere in the vicinity of the next station on the practice tee.

This is one reason why it's more difficult to improve on your own than it is to improve with a coach. You need someone to observe you, to tell you what you're really doing, as opposed to what it feels like you're doing. Even experienced players with excellent, thoroughly understood, swings can use this help. I've stood on the practice tee with Tom Kite and watched him ask Mike Carrick, his caddie, where Tom's club is on his backswing. Sometimes Tom will have Mike hold the shaft of another club at a particular point off Tom's right hip and make certain that his shaft passes over the shaft Mike is holding as he draws the club back. Despite all his years of playing golf, and despite all he knows about his own swing, Tom still isn't precisely certain where his backswing is when he practices. So how can you be? You'd need another pair of eyes.

In making a swing change, of course, the problem is that beyond Tiger Woods and Nick Faldo, few of us can afford to have a teacher next to us each time we practice. Thus, you and your teacher will have to discuss ways to make sure that when you practice your new technique on your own, you're doing it properly.

One method good teachers use is to make certain, during the lesson, that the player gets acquainted with the right feeling. That's why teachers often use an impact bag. It helps players understand what proper hand position at contact feels like.

Another method is based on the principle that Bob Toski's brother Jack used to induce him to change his grip. The teacher devises drills that force the player to perform correctly. Bob may tell a player who has trouble rotating his left arm properly through the hitting zone to spend practice time letting go of the club with the right hand at impact, which forces the left arm to turn properly. There are a thousand drills for all the myriad problems in a golf swing, and any effective effort to change a swing will no doubt use some of them.

•　　•　　•

It will probably help in this effort if you can find ways to practice without a ball.

Wait a minute, you might say. Golf is about hitting a ball and making it go into a hole. Practicing without a ball might seem ridiculous—unless you know Hank Johnson and two of his star pupils, David and Greg Belcher.

I've known Hank for many years. We met at a *Golf Digest* school where he was teaching the swing and I was teaching the mental game. Later on, he moved to Greystone in Birmingham, Alabama.

A few years ago, Hank was struggling with a problem that faces many pros. He had some pupils who didn't have time to practice. They were professional people who were chained to their jobs every day, all day. They wanted to get better, but they wanted to play golf, not practice it, on the weekends.

Hank started to think about ways that these pupils could practice the correct motions at night, at home. He began to devise exercises for them, using some rudimentary, home-made tools. He had them practice the golf swing holding a soccer ball rather than a club in their hands. He had them practice the putting motion without a club or a ball, but with the left hip pressed against the frame of an open door—which forced them to move their hands with their shoulders.

He had each of them build a plane board out of plywood. A plane board, if you're not familiar with it, is simply a flat board about six feet long and three feet high, constructed with legs, so that it can be propped up at any angle to the ground from zero to ninety degrees. A player sets it to the correct angle for the plane of the club he is swinging. He stands behind it and lets the club shaft rest against the front of the board. If he swings along the board, it helps him learn how the correct plane feels.

Hank devised a series of plane-board exercises, most of which the pupil does holding a kitchen broom rather than a golf club. They're all designed to help the player practice the correct motions at different points in the golf swing. I won't go into all of them here because Hank has published a book that includes them, *How to Win the Three Games of Golf*.

Hank was inclined to think of these exercises as poor substitutes for practicing on a range with clubs and balls—until he noticed something. The pupils who had no daylight hours for practice, who worked strictly with the home exercises, were getting better faster than pupils who worked regularly and exclusively on the range.

This puzzled Hank for a while, but the more he thought about it, the more he believed he understood it. He theorized that the act of hitting a golf ball is not necessarily the best way to learn a new swing movement.

When a player hits a golf ball, even a practice ball, he wants to hit it well. He wants to see it fly in the direction he intended. Whether he realizes it or not, he quite often wants that satisfaction more than he wants to execute his new move properly. The feedback for trying to execute the new move properly, after all, may in the beginning be a lousy shot.

Most players with bad swings, Hank knows, have developed ways to compensate for them. If their swing path, for instance, is out-to-in, they may have learned, subconsciously, to try to close the club face as they move it through the hitting zone. Sometimes, this works well enough to produce a decent shot. But they can't do it consistently enough to be good golfers.

On the practice range, a lot of players hit the ball better with their flawed swings and compensating movements than they do with the new movements their teacher is trying to instill. They get, in effect, misleading feedback from the way their balls travel. Consciously or not, they start practicing their bad swings. They make no progress.

Hank's pupils who practiced in their basements and garages, however, had no concern with how a ball traveled. They were focused solely on training to make a new, proper motion. Consequently, they learned it better and faster.

As he studied these results, Hank would occasionally call me and ask whether his thinking was in accord with what researchers in kinesiology and sports psychology were finding as they studied the way the best coaches instill new skills in athletes in all sports. I told him it was.

My good friend Dr. Bob Christina of the University of North Carolina at Greensboro conducts research in how individuals master athletic skills. Along with Dr. Daniel Corcos of Rush Medical College in Illinois, he published his findings in a manual, *Coaches Guide to Teaching Sport Skills*.

Among the things that Bob advocates is breaking a complex skill into smaller parts. You wouldn't, for instance, try to teach a young diver to perform a triple somersault with two full twists all at once. You'd break the movement down. Away from the pool, you'd teach the technique of springing off the board, perhaps using a trampoline and safety ropes. Far from any water, you'd work on somersaulting and twisting. Only when the diver had mastered all of those separately would you ask her to put them all together and try it at a pool.

That, in essence, was what Hank was doing with his home exercises. Each of them focused on a portion of the golf swing.

Bob Christina has also found that fear of failure is a big obstacle to learning new skills. That, too, corresponded to what Hank had learned. Practicing on the driving range introduces an element of anxiety, if only because the golfer wants to see the ball fly properly. That makes him more inclined to fall back on old, imperfect methods rather than stick with new and better, but still awkward, ones. By having his golfers practice at home, without a ball, Hank eliminated that anxiety.

Hank's method also corresponded to other things I'd heard. Julie Inkster, the LPGA star, told me that she learned the golf swing as a girl in a squash court. The late Harvey

Penick liked to have golfers do things like swinging at dandelions with a weed cutter to master the right movements.

Hank has demonstrated the effectiveness of this method with some pupils who have made excellent progress. Two of his best are the Belcher brothers. David and Greg are shortish, athletic guys in their thirties. Davis is a welterweight and Greg a middleweight. They both work in the automobile business with their father and, in that business, they're expected to play a lot of customer golf. They were both decent but not outstanding players, largely self-taught, until a few years ago. David's handicap was 15 and Greg's was 18. Then, they decided they wanted to shoot in the low 70s instead of the high 80s.

They knew Hank from their church, and approached him about taking lessons. "Do you really want to learn this game?" Hank asked them. "Or do you just want to fix a few things and get better?"

Assured that they wanted to learn the game, Hank told them it would be a long process. He gave them each a copy of his book and asked them to clear some space in their garages, basements, or offices for practice gear. Then he installed a plane board and other apparatus for each of them and taught them the exercises they were to perform.

Hank's method, of course, did not rely solely on indoor exercise. Both David and Greg practiced outdoors as well. When they did, though, it tended to be on exercises and drills Hank had devised. He likes his pupils, for instance, to practice hitting short pitches by placing the ball a foot or so inside the T formed by a bunker rake laid flat on the ground. They have to take the club back high to avoid the rake head, and have to swing it straight to avoid the handle. The drill reinforces the method Hank teaches for that shot.

David and Greg continued to play rounds of golf, though generally with each other and not in tournaments. The fact that they were both in the same program helped them. They reinforced each other.

Their progress was sometimes slow and sometimes nonexistent. At their second lesson, Hank changed David's grip and address. When David tried to hit balls with the new grip and posture, he couldn't hit them more than sixty yards. On the course, he couldn't break 100. But he stayed committed.

"We're going to take three steps backward, but when it comes, it will come fast," Hank promised.

It did. Soon both Greg and David showed improvement. But David improved faster. Hank asked, and learned that David was much more faithful than Greg about doing his indoor exercises. As a result, his swing improved faster and with less conscious effort. Greg had to struggle to improve his plane and overcome a tendency to slice.

David can remember many evenings when his wife would come out to the garage and shake her head over what her husband was doing with that broom and that odd-looking board. The payoff has come in vastly improved golf. David now carries a three handicap. His driving accuracy and distance have both improved. He hits more greens and he putts better. Greg is a six. When they play customer golf, they impress the customers.

The ironic thing about what Hank has learned about teaching golf is how few of his pupils take advantage of it. He estimates that perhaps one in 20 people who come to him for lessons undertake his complete program. The rest are looking for a quick fix—and there are none. Swing changes take time and effort.

The things that Bob Christina and Hank Johnson have learned can reduce the time and pain involved. Anyone who is contemplating a major swing change ought to consider their methods. If possible, they should embark on the change in the autumn, after the competitive golf season is done, and do a full winter of indoor work without a ball to make the progress come faster the next spring.

# CHAPTER 9

## BONEFISHING AND OTHER DISTRACTIONS

A year or so ago, a friend of mine named Dick Kreitler was well on his way to a low, single-digit handicap. Then something happened, something which can be very instructive for you.

Dick is a financial consultant who realized about fifteen years ago that modern communications technology meant that you didn't have to live in New York to be a player on Wall Street. He moved to Ketchum, Idaho. There, he managed his own portfolio and those of his clients quite well, well enough that he was able to retire in his early fifties.

He had moved to Ketchum to take advantage of the skiing at Sun Valley. Shortly after he arrived there, he discovered that a golf school was taking up residence in the resort during the summer months. Dick had not played much golf until then, but he took it up, getting his instruction in periodic visits to the golf school. Gradually, skiing paled and golf became his sport. He whittled his handicap down to about 15. When he retired, he wanted to play as much as he could, which meant Florida in the winter. Dick and his wife took a place in Vero Beach and joined the Orchid Island Golf & Beach Club. There, he met teaching pro Mark Heartfield.

Mark is a smart young teacher who was born and raised in Massachusetts. He divides his time between Orchid Island in the winter and Sankaty Head on Nantucket during the summer months. He has some progressive ideas about instruction. He likes pupils who commit to a series of lessons. Once they do, he tries to devote one-third of the lessons to teaching the swing on the practice tee; one-third to teaching the short game; and one-third to playing lessons, emphasizing course management.

When Dick decided to make Mark his teacher, he committed himself to this program. It involved more than just golf lessons. Dick is a stocky, muscular guy, and Mark thought he needed more flexibility, so he introduced him to a physical therapist, Gary Kitchell, who began working with Dick on stretching exercises.

Dick took a golf lesson from Mark every week, and was a model pupil. He practiced diligently, and came to each lesson with an agenda, something he wanted to work on. Mark finds this kind of pupil much more apt to learn than someone who simply shows up and says, "Okay, pro, what do you want to work on today?"

Not surprisingly, Dick improved quickly under this regimen. His short game got a lot sharper. His ball-striking became more consistent, primarily because he and Mark worked on improving his preshot setup, and taking some tension out of his swing. Thanks to the course-management lessons he was taking, Dick made fewer foolish mistakes when he played. As a result, his handicap dropped in the course of one winter season from about 15 to nine.

That's tremendous progress. Dick was playing a lot of rounds in the 70s, and was enjoying golf as never before. He returned to Vero Beach this past winter determined to get even better, and resumed his program with Mark.

This time, he and Mark decided on a swing change. Dick tended to hit a high fade with an upright swing, and he played a lot of his golf in windy places. If you've ever tried to play a high fade on a windy day, you know how difficult it can be. The wind turns fades into slices and makes balls balloon and fall well short of their normal distance. Mark felt that to get his handicap down to the next level, around five, Dick would have to learn to hit a draw with a lower trajectory. To do that, he thought Dick would have to develop a flatter swing plane; that is, the path of the club is somewhat lower and further out behind the player's back.

They started to work on it, and several things happened. First, Dick became quite determined to master the change, which was fine. But his determination caused him to prod Mark to spend more of their lesson time on the practice tee, working on the new swing. They spent less time working on Dick's short game, even though Mark felt there was still ample room for improvement in that area.

Second, Dick's scores started to go up. Orchid Island has water on nearly every hole. It can look tight, even claustrophobic, and can be a tough place to work on a new swing. Dick was hitting more balls into the water. As a result he got a little tight. Mark could see this as they played together. Moves Dick executed on the practice tee didn't come off on the course.

Dick's handicap rose from nine to eleven. At about that time, he discovered bonefishing.

I'm not a fisherman, but I will take the word of Dick and others who testify that it's an exhilarating experience. "It's a riot," Dick says.

Suddenly, he was gone from Orchid Island for weeks at a time on bonefishing trips. His golf practice became sporadic. His progress stopped.

Dick did not consciously think, "My golf isn't going so well, so I'm going to get interested in something else." He just did. It wasn't until recently, upon some reflection, that he decided there was a connection between his rising handicap and his interest in bonefishing.

The connection between Dick's golf swing and his interest in bonefishing is an example of what causes many golfers to fall short of their goals. They stay enthused and committed while they're seeing progress, but their commitment and enthusiasm wane when the progress stops. Since virtually no one makes smooth, steady progress in golf, this helps assure that most people fail to stick with an improvement program.

Mark Heartfield sees this all the time. A lot of the members at Orchid Island are people who suddenly have more time to devote to golf than they ever had before. They've retired, or cut back on their work. They still have their health, and they have the means to take as many lessons and hit as many range balls as they'd like. Of the pupils who come to him, he estimates that about half say they want to embark on a long-term improvement program.

But Mark estimates that only 15 percent stick to it. The rest find that other interests seem more compelling. They've got out-of-town guests. They've got volunteer work. Or, as in Dick's case, they've got some other sport.

What they've got, I think, is a lack of patience. The fact is that you probably won't stay the course if you can't be patient, if only a falling handicap can motivate you.

If you want to stay the course, it will help if you can fall in love not with improvement, but with the process of improvement. Improvement is not something you can tightly control. It will come, but you can't decide when and how much you'll get better.

You can control your immersion in the process of improvement. If you decide that you love striving to get better, you can always make yourself happy by working at your game.

This is what you must do if you expect to honor your commitment.

A good teacher, like Mark Heartfield, will try to help you. Mark does whatever he can to make his lessons fun. He's softspoken and encouraging. When a pupil hits a frustrating patch, he tries to simplify things, to make the changes the pupil is working on easier. But, there is only so much the teacher can do to help you. The rest has to come from within you.

"The people who stick with the program tend to be organized, systematic people," Mark observes. "They have a desire to be better and a love of the game."

And, I think, they love the improvement process.

Dick Kreitler, I am sure, will bounce back. He had the discipline and organization required to work as a financial consultant two thousand miles from New York, getting up every morning at 4:30 to be ready for the opening of the markets. He understands now why he hit a frustrating patch last winter. He understands what he'll have to do if he wants to both improve at his golf and indulge his new love for bonefishing. Mark will try to make sure that he devotes more time to his short game, which ought to improve his scoring.

It's now just a matter of whether he has the patience to stick with it.

CHAPTER 10

# THE PSYCHOLOGY
# OF PRACTICE

Golf is a great social sport. But as I study the habits of great golfers, I'm often struck by how many of them found it a solitary endeavor, especially as they practiced.

The archetype, of course, is Ben Hogan. Whether it was due to the harsh circumstances of his childhood or just a sense of what would help him learn to play golf, Hogan liked being alone. He even had a fictitious alter ego, Henny Bogan, to keep him company.

When Hogan practiced, he went to the far right end of the driving range so that he could turn his back on the rest of the players. I spent some time with Hogan in Ft. Worth several years ago, and I asked him why he did that. He explained that he simply didn't want to watch what anyone else was doing. He was working as hard as he could to monitor and refine what *he* was doing. In the prime of his career, after his swing had become the model for American golf, people often gathered to watch him practice. Hogan, conscious of the fact that he was paid to let people watch him play golf, tolerated this. But he insisted that no one speak to him as he worked. A business executive, he pointed out, would not be expected to tolerate people barging into his office to ask him questions. So, why should a golfer?

I've heard other stories of the way great golfers worked, and solitude is often a part of them. Byron Nelson got his first professional's job in the depths of the Depression. On weekdays, almost no one had the leisure to come out to the club for play or lessons. So Nelson practiced, hitting irons to one end of the practice area, walking after them, and hitting them back. Paul Runyan had a similarly lonely job at a club in Arkansas, and took advantage of it to hone his short game.

Ken Venturi, when he was growing up in San Francisco, had a stammering problem. It was so bad that he was ashamed to play a sport where he might have to talk to his teammates and risk being teased. That was why he took up golf—he could play alone. He spent hours at the practice area in Harding Park, hitting balls and talking to himself. He pretended to be an announcer, describing how his own next shot could decide the Open championship. In fact, he believes that learning the rhythm of the golf swing and harnessing it to his speech was the key to overcoming his stammer.

Mark O'Meara, to take a great player of the present day, has said that from the time he was 13 or so, golf became his best friend.

I don't think it's coincidental that all of these great players liked to practice alone. Practice doesn't have to be a solitary pursuit; in fact, it can be done profitably with a like-minded friend, the way David and Greg Belcher do it. But the great players' penchant for practicing alone can help you understand the difference between practice and quality practice. If you're working hard at your golf game but not getting better, learning this distinction can help you resume improving.

I see too many players who make one or both of two common mistakes in their approach to practice: The first is that they socialize too much on the practice tee. They're chatting about business or the movies or the putt that got away the last time they played. Their minds are not on the golf shots they're practicing. The second common mistake is beating balls. Beating balls is a mindless exercise. There's nothing wrong with mindless exercise if the sport is, say, jogging. If it's golf, your mind has to be on the task at hand. Otherwise, you're liable to be ingraining bad habits.

One way to determine whether you're beating balls is to compare your mental processes on the course and on the range. On the course, I assume, you have a mental routine.

It includes assessing the variables like lie and wind. It also includes picking out a small target. It includes envisioning the ball going to the target, or, if you're not the type of person who graphically envisions things, waiting until your mind is focused on the target and you're confident the ball is going to go there.

If you don't go through each of those mental steps each time you hit a practice shot, you're probably beating balls.

It would be helpful if players went through their full routines, both mental and physical, each time they hit a practice shot. Not many players have the discipline to do this. After all, on the range, the club they want to hit with is usually in their hands already and the lie isn't likely to change much from one shot to the next. And sometimes, you may be working in such a way that your on-course routine is impossible. You may, for example, be using a club laid on the ground to help make sure your alignment is correct. So I don't criticize a player who truncates his physical routine a bit as he practices, as long as he goes through the steps he needs to focus his mind on every shot.

Remember, you're not practicing to be able to hit good shots on the driving range. You're practicing to be able to hit good shots on the last hole of the biggest match of your life. Your dominant habit will show up there, and it had better be a good one.

You'll notice that practicing with this kind of mental discipline takes time. Hogan was legendary for the number of practice balls he hit. Not many people remember that he didn't hit them all at once. He'd hit a small bag and then stop, maybe drink a little water, and think about what he was trying to accomplish. Then he'd hit another small bag.

If you take your time as you practice, and your time is limited, you will hit fewer balls. That's all right. I would rather see a player hit fifty practice shots with his mind focused on every one, than hit two-hundred shots with his mind wandering.

It might help if you try what Ken Venturi found worked for him long ago in Harding Park. It's the same thing that works for a lot of kids who let their imaginations help them as they practice. Try pretending that instead of standing on the range with a seven-iron in your hand, you're standing in the eighteenth fairway at Augusta, 150 yards from the pin, on Sunday afternoon with the Masters on the line. Let yourself really believe it. (Or, if your imagination isn't that supple, pretend you're standing in the final fairway of your own course, 150 yards out, needing par to win two dollars from your best friend.) Prepare for the shot as you would if your imaginary situation were real. Then hit it.

This will have two benefits. It will help focus your mind on your practice shot. And, it will help you prepare for encountering the real situation. The next time you're in the fairway 150 yards out needing a good shot to beat someone, you won't find the situation abnormal.

Another practice habit that good players employ is switching clubs and distances frequently. You may be able to hit pretty good practice drives after you've had the club in your hand for a few minutes, you've warmed up, and you've gotten used to it. However, on the golf course, you never hit a driver twice in a row. You put the club in your hands after you've hit an iron, perhaps a chip or pitch, and a putt or two. That's a different challenge, and it makes sense to practice for it.

A lot of players I've worked with play a course in their imaginations as they practice. They try to envision how the fairway of the first hole would fit on the practice range, and where the hazards would be. Then, they hit their tee shots. They estimate what they'd have left for their second shots and the hazards they'd face. They select a club and hit that shot. If they think their approach would have been short and right, they pull a wedge and pitch the requisite distance.

This, too, makes sense. Hitting balls on the driving range without imagining fairways and hazards and greens is like practicing jump shots without a rim, just bouncing the ball off a backboard. You wouldn't try to improve your jump shot that way and you shouldn't try to improve your golf by hitting aimless practice balls.

Ben Hogan told me that he used the shag caddie to bring the practice range to life. Hogan and his caddie both wanted the caddie to be able to field every shot Hogan hit to him on the first or second bounce. This gave Hogan a small target to aim at. And if, as he worked his way through a bag of 20 balls, he hit 17 right at the caddie, Hogan felt some pressure on the last three to make it a perfect practice bag, which helped him learn habits of concentration that carried over from the range to the golf course.

Seve Ballesteros told me that in the years when he was playing well, he'd always have his clubs strewn about him on the ground when he practiced, because he was always imagining holes and situations and the shots he would need to play them. He believes that it's no coincidence that in recent years, as his play has gotten spotty, he's often found himself on the range with one club in his hand and the rest neatly stowed in his bag. He's been trying to hit perfect shots with one club instead of practicing to play golf.

Imagining a golf course may help you with one of the practice challenges of a player on an improvement program—spending the right amount of time in the trusting mode. As you go through a series of lessons, you're going to be learning some new mechanics. They may involve a significant swing change, or they may be subtler alterations, like an adjustment in your putting stance. But, by virtue of the fact that you're taking lessons, your mind will be engaged to some degree with mechanics.

As I've said, immediately after a lesson, you may want to spend most of your practice time with your mind in the training mode. That is, you consciously think about the new moves you've been taught. You might be hitting the ball with your mind on your swing path or your weight distribution or something else that your pro has suggested you change.

As the time between lessons goes on, you must gradually increase the number of practice shots you take in the trusting mode. That is, you're not thinking about the mechanics of the stroke. You're thinking about your target and the ball getting to that target. On the golf course, your mind should always be in the trusting mode.

On the practice tee, this isn't easy to do if you're trying to learn a new technique and you mishit a couple of shots. Suppose you're trying to cure a slice by drawing the ball. Suddenly, you hit a couple of big left-to-right fades on the practice tee. The temptation is to stop trusting your swing and start trying to fix it. It's a temptation that, most of the time, you must resist. Practice is, after all, intended to rehearse what you want to do on the golf course. If you set out to practice in the trusting mode and revert to trying to fix your swing when you mishit a ball, that's very likely to be what you'll do on the course. Continuing to trust your stroke as you practice is part of the discipline you have to learn.

This is especially true as tournament play approaches. I don't mind if, during the off-season, a player decides to abandon the trusting mode and go back to the practice mode to work on something that doesn't feel quite right. This is especially true if his teacher is around, which is one of the advantages of working with someone from your own club or course. Your teacher might be able to take a quick look at what you're doing and make a suggestion that will fix it on the spot.

But as competition approaches, I advise against trying to fix anything that goes wrong. Within a week of a tournament, you don't have time to fix any fundamental flaws. You want to be training your mind for tournament pressure.

The best thing you can do if you hit a skein of bad shots during pretournament practice is put the club away and go work on some other part of your game. You simply have to believe that you hit the bad shots because you got careless with some part of your routine and that your normal stroke will return once competition starts.

Practicing in the trusting mode will also help you know when you've mastered a new skill. If the shot doesn't work in the trusting mode, then you haven't mastered it: You haven't reached the level of unconscious competence.

Your goal ought to be an overall ratio of roughly six practice shots in the trusting mode for every four shots with your mind focused on technique. So, if you hit all, or nearly all, of your shots in the training mode in the days immediately after your lesson, you ought to be hitting the vast majority of them in the trusting mode as your next lesson draws near.

Your practice plan ought to include a lot of work on the kinds of lies that trouble you. If you're having problems with, say, downhill lies, make sure you go over the adjustments they require with your pro, perhaps during a playing lesson. Then, find a way to practice from that lie. It might mean going out on the course very early in the morning or late in the evening, but I can assure you that the reason good players seem to handle those tricky lies with ease is because they've practiced on them.

They've also practiced with focused minds. As you plan your practice, remember the examples of Hogan, Nelson, and Runyan, as well as some of the modern players I've worked with like Brad Faxon, Davis Love III, Pat Bradley, and Billy Mayfair. Think about ways you can make practice an excursion into your own little world. It might entail practicing at certain times when the facilities on which you practice will be less crowded. It might entail going down to the far end of the range, as Hogan did. However you manage it, practicing with a focused mind will make your practice more efficient and beneficial.

How much should you practice? It depends, of course, on the time and enthusiasm you have.

Bill Davis has a couple of pupils, Jay and Arline Hoffman, who have decided they want to see how good they can get at golf and are prepared to devote a lot of time to it.

Jay started out in golf in a way that taught him to associate the sport with hard work—as a caddie. At Washington Golf & Country Club in northern Virginia in the mid-1950s, caddies got $2.50 per bag and maybe a fifty-cent tip for walking a hilly course in the fetid humidity that is Washington in the summer. If he carried two bags for two rounds, he could earn maybe $11 for a day's work. After a couple of years of caddying, he switched to carrying bricks at construction sites. After serving in the army, he went into the construction business. He played golf a bit, with his caddie's swing, but not often enough to get good at it.

Over the years, though, Jay reached the stage where he owned enough real estate and radio stations to begin to set his own schedule. He and Arline started spending a lot of their time in Florida and they joined Jupiter Hills Golf Club.

Arline had never played until her child went off to college, but when she took it up, she found she liked the challenge of controlling the golf ball. They began taking a joint weekly lesson from Bill Davis.

When he gets pupils who are eager to learn and willing to put time into the effort, Bill will prescribe their practice sessions, writing down the shots he wants them to try. Here is what one of Jay and Arline's recent practice regimens looked like:

1. PUTTING:

   **a.** Seven-point compass drill from one, two, three, four and five feet, five times per week.

   **b.** Putting with eyes closed, three balls from three, six, and nine feet, seven repetitions, five times per week. (This drill is intended to focus the pupil's attention on how hard he's hitting the putt, not on his line or putting mechanics.)

**c.** Putting from one cup to another set 20 feet apart, ten repetitions, five times per week.

2. CHIPPING:

**a.** From three yards off the green with seven-iron, nine-iron, pitching wedge, and sand wedge, five with each club, five times per week.

**b.** The same drill from six yards off, eliminating the seven-iron and adding a lob wedge, five times per week.

**c.** The same drill from nine yards off, using the three wedges, five times per week.

3. SHORT PITCHES:

**a.** From 15 yards off the green with the three wedges, five balls each, five times per week.

**b.** Same drill from 20 yards, five times per week.

**c.** Same drill from 25 yards, five times per week.

4. LONGER PITCHES:

**a.** From 50 yards, five balls each with pitching wedge and sand wedge, five times per week

**b.** The same drill from 60 yards, five times per week.

**c.** The same drill from 70 yards, five times per week.

5. BUNKER PLAY:

**a.** 15 shots each with the sand wedge and the lob wedge from different lies in the practice bunker, five times per week.

6. FULL SWING:

**a.** 10 balls each with nine-iron, seven-iron, five-iron, a fairway wood and a driver, two repetitions, three times per week.

This means that in a week's time, Jay and Arline would each hit 300 long shots, 590 putts, and 795 chips and pitches. Bill anticipates that they'll also play four rounds of golf per week and take two days off to keep fresh.

Not surprisingly, the Hoffmans have improved by following this regimen. Jay, who was a 22-handicapper when he started with Bill a few years ago, recently played 12 consecutive rounds in the 70s. Arline's handicap has dropped to about 12.

"We like to practice," Jay says. "And we have faith in Bill. We know what he's teaching us will help us."

This is a strong practice schedule and I realize that not everyone can take this sort of time, but it's exemplary in several respects. First, it places proper emphasis on the short game. Second, it's a plan that Bill and Jay and Arline have mutually agreed on, even though Bill takes the role of prescribing the drills and shots he wants them to practice. They all believe it will help them. And, finally, the Hoffmans enjoy it.

It's important to try to make practice enjoyable. For some people, this is not a problem. They love getting out to practice and they'll do it in the rain if necessary. For others, it's a partial problem. They like certain kinds of practice—perhaps hitting drivers—but they don't care for others, like putting.

This is where a buddy system of the sort that Jay and Arline have may be helpful. I know I've pointed out the solitary practice habits of many great golfers, but remember that they sought solitude not for its own sake but because it helped them focus and concentrate as they practiced.

Two people can do this as effectively, perhaps more effectively, than one—if they're both committed to the same program. They can reinforce one another. They can prod one another. When they practice together, they're not socializing. There's a sense of companionship, of camaraderie, that comes from being engaged in a joint enterprise, but they're both concentrating on the task at hand.

David and Greg Belcher, Hank Johnson's star students, have this sort of relationship. They compete with one another, but they both take pride and pleasure in the other's achievements. When they play a round of golf together, each urges the other to stick with the techniques Hank has shown them, even if those techniques are as yet unpolished and are not helping their score on this particular day. Jay and Arline play together in much the same way.

If two people are supposed to practice, it may increase the likelihood that they'll do it. If one is not in the mood, the other may prod him to practice anyway. You'll have to decide, based on your own personality and circumstances, whether the buddy system is right for you.

There's one other way that effective practice can involve more than one person. I like to see players compete with one another on the practice green or at the practice tee. If one of your friends happens to be working on his putting at the same time you are, it's fine to make a little bet on who can hole more putts from a given spot. If you're on the range, compete to see who can hit an iron closest to the various target pins that are out there.

You'll be doing what practice ought to do: focusing your mind in the same way you want to focus it on the golf course. That is quality practice.

CHAPTER 11

# WHEN YOU NEED
# ANOTHER TEACHER

One of the first mentor-pupil relationships I ever observed in golf involved a girl named Kandi Kessler and a young teaching pro named Phil Owenby. They taught me something important about handling one of the most difficult and sensitive aspects of anyone's relationship with a teacher. They showed how to bring another teacher into the improvement process constructively.

Kandi took up golf when she was 11 or 12 years old. Up until that time, horses were the love of her life, but she developed some allergies and her doctor told her she couldn't hang around barns any more. To fill the void, her father, Frank, introduced her to golf.

Kandi took to it with passion. She was a shy girl and liked the fact that she could play golf alone.

Her Dad would drop her off in the mornings at Farmington Country Club in Charlottesville, Virginia, and she'd spend the day there. She'd start on the practice range, move to the practice green, then head for east nine, the least played of Farmington's 27 holes. She'd play it two, three, sometimes four times, then she'd hit balls until it got dark.

Within a year or two, she could shoot in the 80s. She had a few lessons that helped her with the fundamentals of grip and posture, but had no regular mentor until Phil Owenby came along.

Phil is a tall, soft-spoken golfer from North Carolina. He'd played college golf at N.C. State, but when he went up against Curtis Strange and Jay Haas, who were over at Wake Forest, he realized teaching would be his niche in the game.

The day after graduation, Phil started working as an intern in the pro shop at Farmington, doing the things people do on the bottom rung of the teaching ladder—looking after the range, the carts, and the bag room. He soon noticed Kandi.

"She had a thirst to get better," he recalls now, nearly twenty years later. "So we hit it off."

This is an important factor in the forging of a strong relationship between any pro and any golfer. If the pro is convinced the golfer has that thirst to do better, that will to work, he or she will naturally respond more favorably than to someone who conveys a lackadaisical attitude. It's one of the things that separates good players from average players.

Good players have a knack of showing teachers that they're eager to improve. One of your jobs as a player is to make sure your teacher knows how much you want to get better.

Phil started tutoring Kandi. On summer evenings, after his regular work was done, they'd take a cart out onto the east nine. She drove, which is always a treat for a youngster. Their lessons were not unlike the ones Bill Davis gives to Patty Pilz. As they played, Kandi would sometimes hit her ball into difficult situations—deep rough, uneven lies—and Phil would teach her how to cope with them. Sometimes he'd let her hit several balls from each spot. Sometimes he'd ask her to play with one ball and they'd try to get a lot of holes in before dark.

"She was a natural mimic," Phil recalls. He only had to show her something once or twice and she would start to incorporate it into her own game. Teaching on the course that way kept it fun for her, he remembers. It also taught her to think about things like shot trajectory, working the ball left or right, and course management.

They worked on her swing as well. Kandi had a tendency to take the club back too far inside, and Phil gave her drills designed to prompt her to make a more upright swing. Sometimes he would have her swing with her rear end against a wall. Sometimes he'd put a club behind her on the practice tee and and she'd try to take her club back toward the club on the ground behind her.

Under this tutelage, Kandi improved dramatically. Her

handicap dropped from the high teens to two or three by the time she was a junior in high school. She won the state junior amateur three times. When she was 16, she won the state amateur. She started thinking seriously about a career on the LPGA Tour. Around this time, I started helping her with her mental game.

Kandi and her father decided that if she were going to play professionally, she would need a better short game than she had. They wanted her to get it from the best instructors available. They tried a couple, and then I suggested they talk to Davis Love, Jr.

But we never cut Phil Owenby out of this process or did anything behind his back. He was consulted. The Kesslers invited him to come along with them to Sea Island, Georgia, where Davis Love, Jr., taught.

Phil, at this point, could have declined and bowed out, but he was smart enough to realize that as a young and relatively inexperienced teacher, he could learn a lot from someone like Davis Love, Jr. So he went with the Kesslers.

He absorbed an enormous amount just by watching Kandi's lessons.

"The first thing I learned was how he handled people," Phil recalls. "He'd have Kandi hit balls for maybe 15 or 20 minutes, not saying anything, until she started to relax. He had a way of making her feel very good about herself. When he was about to teach her something, he'd start off by saying, 'This will be easy for you, as good an athlete as you are.'"

Davis Love, Jr., taught both Phil and Kandi things they hadn't known about the short game. Once, it was a discourse on the design of the various wedges, how they're supposed to penetrate turf and sand. On another occasion it was a discussion of controlling the distance on short pitches by varying the length of the backswing, allowing the downswing always to be firm and accelerating.

Whatever he taught, he was always supportive of Phil. "He'd always be saying, 'When you go back, Phil should work with you on this or that,'" Phil recalls.

"I think Mr. Love actually liked having Phil watch the lessons, because I lived so far away from Sea Island," Kandi remembers. "He knew somebody would be reinforcing what he taught me and I'd have less tendency to revert to old habits."

Kandi went on to become a Curtis Cup player for the United States. She played in five U.S. Opens, finishing fourteenth in her best year. She turned pro and had some success, but eventually opted to give up touring in order to marry and have a family. Now Kandi Kessler-Comer, she's the director of golf at Glenmore Country Club near Charlottesville, the same post Phil occupies at Roanoke Country Club. They stay in touch.

The kind of candid, constructive relationship they had is all too rare. Too often, if someone decides to see another pro, he does so secretly. Maybe he thinks his regular pro will be angry or offended at the implied lack of confidence. Maybe he just wants to avoid a conversation he fears could be unpleasant. Doubt and confusion usually ensue. A player seeing two teachers tends to tune out what the older teacher says to him. The relationship of trust they once had is spoiled.

No two pros, even two pros who agree on the fundamentals of the swing, teach the same. They have differences of nuance, differences of emphasis, differences, perhaps, of terminology. The player who sees two or more pros will inevitably zero in on whatever slight differences exist between them. Right away, he loses some confidence in his swing. How can he trust his swing when he hears, or thinks he's hearing, two different ways to do it? He can't. A player who doesn't trust his mechanics swings tentatively, stiffly, gracelessly. His results get worse. Pretty soon, he's lost.

This can be a big problem for some of the tour players I work with. Of necessity, they're on the road a lot, away from their swing teachers, and the practice tees at tour events are full of people who would like to make a reputation as a teacher by giving tips to a star. They're full of fellow playing pros, many of them well-meaning, who know a lot about the swing and are all too happy to share what they know.

A player who misses a cut or two is tempted to start listening to this free advice. Or he hears about Teacher X, who's helped a certain player turn his fortunes around. There are vogues in golf teaching, and there is always someone who seems anointed, for the moment at least, as the man who knows the secret.

My friend Brad Faxon worked through a problem of this sort early in 1997. Brad's 1996 season was, by most standards, a fine one. He finished second in four tournaments and eighth on the money list and led the tour in putting. But he didn't win an event, and he was down the list in driving statistics. Brad wanted to improve his long game and he worked hard at it.

Early in 1997, though, his hard work wasn't paying off. He missed a couple of cuts in California and Florida. When his long swing wasn't grooved perfectly, he fretted about it. He started listening to too much advice on mechanics. He got a bit confused.

We talked before the Player's Championship in late March. I suggested a few things to Brad. I thought he needed to go back to the basics of his game. While it was fine to try to improve his long swing, he had to remember that no one swings perfectly. He had to remember that wedges and putting are the strengths of his game and he should enjoy using them. He had to filter out the conflicting advice he was getting and settle on one method, and only one method, to believe in.

When Brad did that, he went on a tear. He finished fourth at the Players' Championship, won at New Orleans, tied for second at Hilton Head, was second at Greenboro, and tied for second at the Colonial. In a single month, he won hundreds of thousand of dollars and put himself in a strong position to make the Ryder Cup team. Setting aside doubt and confusion helped him do it.

The need to avoid doubt and confusion must guide you as well.

It's not outside the realm of possibility that you will reach a point where the advice of another pro can be helpful to you. After all, no one goes through an academic education with just one teacher. In kindergarten and the primary grades, one teacher can handle all subjects. By the time high school begins, a student goes to different teachers, each of whom specializes in a different subject. If he goes to college or graduate school, he may have a particular faculty member who serves as his advisor. However, that teacher's job may include referring the student to other teachers and courses for the knowledge he needs.

It may be that after you've progressed beyond the golfing equivalent of elementary school, you'll feel a need for specialized instruction in some facet of the game—wedge play, perhaps, or psychology. You'll want to consult specialists. If you're serious about becoming a tournament player, perhaps a touring pro, you may need to put together a team of sorts: a primary teacher; perhaps a fitness expert to help with strength and flexibility; a sport psychologist to help with your mental game; and maybe one or two specialized teachers.

If and when that happens, be smart. Handle it as Kandi Kessler and her father did when they decided she needed some specialized short game instruction from Davis Love, Jr. Talk it over with your regular teacher. You may be surprised at his reaction. He may agree with you. He may have some good ideas about people to consult. He may even be willing to go with you and observe your lessons. He ought to be willing to review any videotape you bring back from the lesson.

Whatever happens, share with your teacher the things you learn from the specialist. Let him help you integrate them into the game you've been building. Even if your principal teacher and the specialist disagree about how to hit a particular shot or perform a particular part of the swing, and you decide to take the specialist's advice, tell your principal teacher what you're doing and why. You'll still need his help and guidance and he'll be in a better position to give it if you keep him informed.

There's always a possibility, when bringing in new teachers, that egos will collide. Everyone involved with a golfer ought to realize that they're in it not to enhance their own reputations and egos, but to help the player. Unfortunately, that's not always the case.

Not all teachers and consultants know what Bear Bryant knew about apportioning credit. When Bryant's Alabama teams won big, he always told the press that the boys played well. When Alabama lost, he always took the blame for himself. That's one reason he was a great coach.

If not everyone you're working with is as instinctively wise as Bear Bryant, you have a management problem. The last thing you need is to have one teacher disparaging the other, trying to undermine someone else. The best way to avoid this is to be open with everyone you work with and demand that they integrate their advice into the package you're putting together.

# CHAPTER 12

## PARENTS AND CHILDREN

The man may wear his cap with the peak turned out over his forehead, the way the designer intended, while the boy's cap is turned backward, the way baseball catchers wear them. The man may wear his trousers cinched with a proper belt, while the boy's shorts droop fashionably low, hanging precariously between his hips and his shins. The man may hum snatches from a Beach Boys tune as he walks while the boy whistles something from Fugazi.

But, if they are playing golf together, they are, for a while at least, comrades.

Few things in our culture can bridge the gap between generations as well as golf. It's a game that fathers and mothers introduce to their sons and daughters. It's a game that families can play together when the kids are growing up and after the kids are grown and have kids of their own.

The link between generations doesn't even have to be from older to younger. I helped my own father and mother take up golf when they were in their sixties. Now, some of the most pleasant time we spend together is on a golf course.

It's hard to think of an outstanding golfer of the past half century or so, from Arnold Palmer and Jack Nicklaus down through Pat Bradley and Davis Love III, whose game was not intertwined in a close, loving relationship with a father.

Most often, what I hear these players say when they talk about the contributions their fathers made to their games has nothing to do with the grips they passed on, or the backswings. It has to do with character. Jack Nicklaus recounts how his father cured him of throwing clubs. Davis Love III talks about how his dad taught him to be honest about reporting his scores. "Pap didn't just teach me how to play golf," Arnold Palmer once said. "He taught me discipline."

So, if you teach your children to love golf and to play it well, you're not just giving them a game that can reward them with pleasure and exercise for the rest of their lives. You have an opportunity to teach traits like honor, discipline, and perseverance that will help them in whatever they do.

It's not as simple as having a child, cutting down some clubs, and doing what comes naturally. I've seen athletes whose careers and lives were damaged by parents who didn't know where to draw the line between support and interference, between loving and smothering, between encouraging and pushing. I'm sympathetic toward them, because there can be no clear rules about where that line ought to be. Each child is different—what seems pushy and smothering to one child may seem warm and supportive to another.

I'm working right now with a young man, Mike Henderson, whose father, Dan, has been very active in his golfing development. When he was 16, Mike was selected the Rolex Junior Golfer of the Year from a field that included Tiger Woods, so he and Dan must be doing something right.

Mike is the youngest by ten years of Dan and Glenda Henderson's four children. By the time he turned ten, the other children were more or less out of the nest. Dan, who has a business distributing vitamins, was then in a financial position to set his own schedule.

One day when Mike was 10 years old, Dan cut down a club and took him to a driving range. Dan, who carried about a four handicap, taught his son a few of the fundamentals of grip, stance, and swing; Mike started popping straight shots into the range.

None of his other children had become serious golfers, but Dan saw potential in Mike, and he immediately began to cultivate it.

They were, in fact, getting a late start. Lots of juniors start much earlier. About a month after he played his first round of golf, Mike entered a junior tournament, the North State, at his home course, North Ridge Country Club in Raleigh, North Carolina.

"How many tournaments you played in?" Mike's playing partner asked.

"This is my first," Mike said, politely.

"I've played in about a hundred," the other 11-year-old said. "Know how many trophies I've won?"

"How many?"

"About a hundred," the kid said.

Unintimidated, Mike shot a 92 and finished fifth.

Mike and his father were just getting started. Dan started coming home early from work, picking up Mike at school. They lived near the seventh green at North Ridge, and there was a six-hole loop that began near their back door. They played it every night, but they did more than play holes. They stopped around idle greens and chipped and putted extra balls. They practiced.

Dan did not want Mike just hanging around the club. "My philosophy was to help him get good fairly quickly," Dan recalls. "But parents who just drop their kids off at the club aren't doing that. Those kids' first focus is social. They don't get better."

Dan gave up his own golf game in favor of supervising Mike's. "Most parents choose to spend their time playing themselves or drinking at the nineteenth hole," he says. "I chose to spend it with Mike. I was there enough that he could stay focused."

Dan did not try to be Mike's swing teacher. He sought out good instruction. He first took Mike to Austin, Texas to see Mike Adams. There was a trip to Florida to see Jimmy Ballard and a trip to Maryland to see Kent Cayce at Congressional Country Club.

Mike was improving rapidly. At the age of 12, he shot a couple of rounds in the sixties, from the red tees. He's a pleasant, teachable kid, and he learned from each of the pros he and his father went to see. He practiced what they showed him, under Dan's watchful eye. Dan videotaped his lessons so they could refer back to them if some question arose.

Dan was still not satisfied they had found the teacher they could commit to. He read an article about David Leadbetter in *Golf Digest,* tracked down Leadbetter's phone number, and persuaded David's wife to schedule a one-hour lesson for Mike, even though David at that time was not taking new students. When Dan sees something he wants, he is not easily deterred. When the time came, he and Mike drove ten hours to Orlando.

The one-hour lesson stretched to five hours. Both Dan and Mike liked the way David analyzed his swing and liked even more the way he helped Mike correct his flaws. "I knew I was home if David would work with Mike," Dan recalls.

It was not easy to get a commitment from David, who could easily work 24 hours a day with all the golfers who would like to take lessons from him. For a couple of years, they saw David occasionally, but took lessons from other teachers. Finally, they reached an agreement. David would see Mike every month or six weeks, and he would review videotapes Mike sent him.

From that point, David has been Mike's only swing teacher. Mike has been a conscientious pupil. David, for example, taught Mike to check on his setup position in a mirror. Mike has faithfully stood in front of a mirror for 15 minutes or so each day, practicing getting into the correct posture. He's developed a beautiful golf game.

The important thing is not that Mike has worked with David Leadbetter, although David is certainly a great teacher. The important thing is that he found a teacher he believed in, he committed himself to taking instruction only from that teacher, and he has faithfully done what the teacher has asked.

Dan, for his part, did what fathers need to do in this process. He recognized his son's potential and desire to improve. He found his son a teacher he believed in, and he let the teacher teach. Dan observes Mike's lessons and makes the videotapes, but he would never try to contradict something David has taught Mike. His role is to support David when David isn't there.

This is the right approach for a parent to take. Parents ought to lay down certain rules of behavior for their young golfers. They ought to require that a child meet minimal standards for behavior, temper, sportsmanship, and grades in school if he or she is to continue playing and taking lessons. But they ought not try to teach the backswing.

Dan took on another role on Mike's behalf. Mike is naturally a warm, friendly, and personable kid, the kind of kid who will politely chat with anyone about golf. Once he started to win junior championships, he became something of a celebrity. People wanted to talk to him when they saw him on the range. They wanted him to explain what he was doing, and they wanted him to watch what they were doing. Mike didn't have what Ben Hogan had, that ability to get curt when he had to practice.

So, Dan became the watchman. He accompanied Mike when he practiced. He diverted the people who wanted to talk to Mike. They could talk to Dan.

"A lot of people thought that I was standing over Mike, making him practice," Dan says. "I never had to make him practice. I just had to make sure he had a chance to practice."

Still, it was a tight relationship between an adolescent boy and his father and there were times when it chafed. The Hendersons got through those times with love and good communication. Dan has always allowed Mike to voice any complaint that he has.

"There were times when I'd get angry with him or he'd get angry with me, but I always knew it was never something important enough to sacrifice our relationship," Mike says. "You understand that you both love and care for each other, and you get over it."

As Mike grew older, Dan stepped back a bit. "From the time he was about 16, I was there less," Dan recalls. This is a natural step, but one that some parents and children understandably find difficult. Almost of necessity these days, a parent is going to be heavily involved in the development of a young golfer. There are almost no caddie yards anymore where kids can learn the game on their own.

But there will come a time, in the midteens, when the parent–child relationship has to change and become more collegial. The parent has to start doing less talking and more listening. The child has to have room to grow up.

For Dan Henderson, the hardest part was seeing Mike go off to college. Mike chose Brigham Young University, a couple of thousand miles from home, because he liked the campus atmosphere, and because his coach there was happy to let David Leadbetter remain the only one to correct Mike's swing. The Hendersons, who are Mormons, were happy with the choice, but there are times, when Dan knows Mike is playing in a tournament out west, when he finds it hard not to be there.

Mike has done well at BYU. He was Western Athletic Conference freshman of the year in 1996, and was first-team all conference in 1997. He aspires to win some major amateur events, and then make his mark on the PGA Tour.

He knows what he has to do to accomplish that. Mike is not a big guy. His tee shots average about 260 yards, and he won't outmuscle anyone at the professional level. His success will depend on how sharp he gets with the scoring clubs, particularly the putter. It's a big jump from junior golf to the tour.

The Hendersons' development formula might not be suitable for everyone. A child who wasn't instantly passionate about golf might not be able to accept, as Mike did, Dan's level of involvement—and certainly not every child needs to take lessons from David Leadbetter.

There are two key things in the upbringing of any junior golfer that the Hendersons did right, that are appropriate for anyone. Dan found his son a teacher they both believed in, a teacher who could credibly promise to take Mike to the level he sought. Later, as Mike became competitive at the national level, Dan sought out other experts to help with other aspects of his development. That's when I became Mike's sports psychologist. Dan, though he was always present, never dominated Mike, never forced him to do anything.

Any junior who travels to tournaments is going to have a parent for a companion, and that parent had better let the child voice his or her opinion. That parent should respect the child's opinion to the degree that the child's maturity warrants, and facilitate, not block, the child's desire to make friends with the other kids.

Otherwise, the outcome might not be as good as it was with Mike Henderson. The outcome could be burnout and the loss of the opportunity to enjoy the benefits that golf can bring to the relationship between a parent and a child.

CHAPTER 13

# THE MONEY FACTOR

Here are two truths about the relationship between money and the golf of your dreams:

You can't buy a game.

You can't learn for free, either.

There are indeed people who act as if they think they can buy a game. They go to golf schools at resorts where the range attendants wear white gloves. They buy all the best things: clubs, balls, clothes, gadgets. The first time some company comes out with a ten-thousand dollar driver, they'll buy that, too.

Their spending by itself won't make them much better, if at all. While it's nice to have good equipment, the fact is that good players can shoot par with the old set of rusted MacGregors they inherited from Uncle Jack and stashed in the garage on the off chance that they might one day be antiques.

There are also people who let money keep them away from the kind of improvement that would make the game more enjoyable for them. They're not about to pay some golf pro fifty dollars for a lesson, to say nothing of one hundred fifty dollars.

If they're the sort of people who play a few times a year on days when the greens fees are discounted, that's fine—so long as they know that their golf budget is constraining their ability to play well, and they accept that fact.

However, there are lots of people who fall somewhere between these two extremes. Their means are not unlimited, yet they spend a fair amount of money on the game by the time you add up their club dues, their new irons, their fresh Titleists, their vacation tabs at nice golf resorts, their greens fees. They spend a lot of time on the game, too. They want to improve, but they balk at spending money or time on a systematic improvement program.

All I can say to them is that they ought to decide how much getting better at golf is worth to them. If they have to work within a budget, should their priority be a new set of irons or learning how to play better?

The cost of improvement is substantial but not outlandish. Short-game practice costs nothing. Range balls aren't too expensive. There are lots of good teachers like Gene Hilen out there, giving lessons for twenty-five dollars. And, if you come to a pro ready to commit yourself to a series of lessons, you're in a decent bargaining position. Most pros will offer you some kind of package rate.

If you're a parent looking for lessons for your child, be aware that most teaching pros are delighted to come across a child with a little talent and a hunger to learn and practice. They are often willing to cut some deals that can reduce the cost of lessons to almost nothing, especially if the child is old enough to do odd jobs, like picking balls up off the range or cleaning clubs.

All in all, it should be possible to pay for a three-month improvement cycle for about what it takes to play a single round of golf at Pebble Beach. You could spend a lot more. You could probably spend a little less.

What is it worth to you?

CHAPTER 14

# THE DISCIPLINE
# YOU'LL NEED

When Rocco Mediate walked out to the tee for a shoot-out exhibition prior to the Las Vegas Classic in the autumn of 1993, he had no inkling that he was about to both alter his career and demonstrate the key to self-discipline. His only intention was to have a good time and maybe win a little money in an event the tour put on for the customers kind enough to buy tickets for practice rounds.

But, when Rocco hit his three-wood off the tee on number 16 that afternoon, he felt a twinge just below the middle of his back. He told his caddie that something didn't feel right, and by the end of the round, he was limping a little bit. A couple of days later, he could barely walk. He withdrew from the tournament.

Rocco had qualified to play in the Tour Championship the following week at the Olympic Club in San Francisco, and he did not want to miss that. On Monday of that week he felt all right. He began to believe that his back pain had been just some kind of sprain. But after 14 holes of his practice round, the pain returned. It was almost unbearable. On the fifteenth tee, he hit a seven-iron toward the green, but it went no more than 120 yards. It took him an hour to hobble the three-hundred yards or so to the clubhouse.

I'll condense what Rocco went through for the next eight months. Anyone who's had a herniated disk knows the story. He consulted specialists. He tried to rehabilitate his back through exercise. There were occasions when the pain eased, and he was able to play. There were times of debilitating agony. He had to call the Masters and withdraw. He managed to play in the U.S. Open at Oakmont, where he was paired with Arnold Palmer in Palmer's last Open. After three rounds, he had to withdraw.

He had back surgery a month after the Open. When he awoke from the anaesthesia, his surgeon told him the operation had gone well. A portion of the disk had been removed, but the nerves in the spine were undisturbed.

That was not the way Rocco felt. The pain from the disk area was gone, but he felt an intense, overarching pain from the surgery, and his back felt stiff, as if encased in something. For a few moments, he doubted he would ever play golf again.

He put that thought aside and started working on his surgeon's plan for rehabilitation. The first thing on the list was six weeks of rest. Rocco complied. He did nothing more active than walk during that period.

As soon as he could, he began working with a trainer, Frank Novakoski. At first, it was a matter of being rubbed down and trying to break up some of the scar tissue that had formed around his spine. But fairly soon, Rocco was on a four-hours-per-day exercise regimen.

I should add here that before his injury, Rocco was not, by his own account, in very good shape. When he won at Greensboro in 1993, he weighed about 245 pounds, and he stands just a little over six feet. He had always figured if he was in shape to walk the golf course, that was good enough.

His initial, presurgery attempts to rehab the disk injury got him into somewhat better condition, but his postsurgery workouts transformed him. The hours of abdominal exercises, stretching and flexibility exercises, stair-climbing exercises, a stationary bike, and other workouts took five or six inches off his waist and about 45 pounds off his body.

He still had lots of work to do before he could play competitive golf again. The first time he was allowed to pick up a club, he took an iron into the back yard and tried to chip a ball about 10 yards, from the kids' swing set to the porch. It hurt so much that he fell to his knees.

He persisted. Six weeks later, he played, and not badly, in the Diner's Club matches. He went to Peter Kostis and Gary McCord for help in changing his swing to place less strain on his back.

He became a regular denizen of the fitness trailer that moves along with the players from tour stop to tour stop. To help motivate himself, he put together a tape of music from the *Rocky* movies. When he played that tape, he could hear some muted snickers. He used them as motivation. "Go ahead and keep laughing, boys," Rocco would say to himself. "I'll step all over you when I go past you."

He nearly lost his card because he won very little money in 1995. He got a medical extension and needed to win quickly as the 1996 season began. He responded brilliantly, winning $42,088 with a sixth-place finish at Phoenix to assure his place on the tour. He went on to finish fortieth on the 1996 money list. Rocco has not yet regained the form he had before his back injury. He's sometimes depressed and frustrated, but he's getting there.

The key to Rocco's recovery, I think, could be discerned in his answer when a journalist asked him whether he had ever thought about what he would do for a living if he couldn't play golf again.

"I never thought about doing anything else," Rocco replied. "I didn't have time."

Now this is a man who, many people would think, had nothing but time to think about a future without competitive golf. He had six weeks of enforced rest after surgery. He had all those hours on the stationary bike and other exercise equipment, but in Rocco's recollection, he had no time.

That, I think, is why he stuck so religiously to his rehabilitation program. His mind was dominated by a vision of himself back on the tour, playing great golf. With that image in front of him, he did his exercises. When his career encountered a crisis, Rocco found that he had the self-discipline, the will, to do what he had to do.

In my experience, self-discipline is not a quality, like blue eyes, that people either have or don't have at birth. Every time they face a situation requiring discipline, people either talk themselves into sticking with a plan or they talk themselves out of it.

Rocco talked himself into it.

You might think that it's easier for a professional athlete, whose livelihood is at stake, to find the discipline he needs to stick with a regimen, but I could show you examples of dozens of athletes who didn't have the discipline to rehabilitate after surgery and who cut their careers short. Mickey Mantle was one.

Money wasn't the motivation you might think. Rocco had put himself and his family in a solid financial position. He was well established as a golfer, and he would have found ways to make a living in the game if his back had prevented him from returning to the tour.

What motivated and still motivates Rocco was his vision. He sees himself winning golf tournaments again. People who can retain that vision, that image of the self they want to be, tend to remain on improvement regimens. People who lose faith in that vision tend to give up, usually after two to eight weeks, once the initial burst of enthusiasm has faded. That's the way it is with most New Year's resolutions.

That's because most improvement programs, if they have any validity at all, produce an immediate, beneficial impact for someone who has, until he begins the program, been floundering.

If you, for example, are an average golfer and you begin the program I've outlined, you'll probably notice some quick results. Your short game will improve because you've begun taking lessons and practicing it. Your course management will improve as well. Your scores will be lower. But somewhere in those first few months, you'll hit your first plateau. You may even, as Dick Kreitler did, find that your scores are going up again as you work to master a swing change.

That's when your discipline will be tested, as Rocco's was.

You'll find, after some discouraging round, that you're beginning to wonder whether the effort you're putting in is worth it. You might have played against someone who never practices, never takes a lesson, but who nevertheless beat you.

You think, *Why should I spend all this time on lessons and practice? I'm always going to be a hacker. All of my friends are going to see me working, and not getting better, and they'll kid me.*

That's when your discipline starts to break down. You put aside the vision of yourself as a fine golfer, a scratch golfer. Instead, you choose to see yourself as duffer. You start to believe that talent determines golfing ability, and that you have no talent. You are on the way to talking yourself out of your commitment to improvement. It becomes easy to find a reason to skip the next practice session, to cancel the next lesson. Very soon, you're back where you started.

Real talent is not what most people think it is. It's not a natural ability to hammer the ball down the range. It's not some extraordinary gift for putting. Real talent is what Rocco displayed when he hurt his back. Real talent is patience. It's persistence. It's the ability always to keep in mind the vision of yourself as you want to be. Real talent leads to discipline, and discipline leads to a sustained effort over a long period of time. That effort is what produces, in the end, long drives down the middle and extraordinary putts.

Everything in this book is designed to help you tap your real talent, to find the discipline you need to get better. If you follow the program, you will have a mentor, your pro, who will help you through the rough spots. You will be working on aspects of the game that will improve your scoring.

But the pro can't learn the game for you. He can teach you, but you must learn it for yourself. That's one of the great things about the game.

Just as I can guarantee that if you stick with this plan for three years, you will play the golf of your dreams, I can guarantee that you will encounter, during those three years, periods when it all seems useless and you're tempted to give up, when other claims on your time suddenly seem more important.

That's when you will have to find the strength within

yourself to stay the course. That's when you have to keep your dream in the front of your mind. That's when you have to arm yourself with reasons to continue.

If you can do that, then, like Rocco Mediate, you can talk yourself into being disciplined.

CHAPTER 15

# A Philosophy of Golf
# and Life

Why should you begin the program I've out-lined? Why should you commit yourself to it? Why persevere in that commitment?

The answer, I think, lies partly in the nature of human beings. To be fully human is to struggle with adversity, to overcome it. A few generations ago, our ancestors faced challenges that were simple and primal. If they wanted to eat, they had to plant crops, work the soil with their hands, and hope that the rains came. If they wanted shelter, they had to cut trees and build it. If they wanted to go somewhere, they had to walk. They survived because they thrived on challenges. If they had not been this way, if their first reaction to a challenge was to roll over and give up, they would have perished before they got a chance to *become* ancestors.

It's reasonable to think that they passed this trait, this tendency to confront and overcome challenges, along to us. We humans are beings with an innate need to be challenged.

But humans also love play. You may have to work to teach a child to read or pick up his room. You generally don't have to work to teach her to play. It comes naturally.

I think this has to do with the natural unity between body and mind. Our modern culture tends to separate the mind from the body. Much of what we do is categorized as either mental work or physical work. In fact, people sometimes ask me where the mind ends and the body begins. They think there must be a point, somewhere between the jawbone and the collarbone, where this separation occurs.

I don't think they are separate, and I think we we are most content when our minds and bodies are working in harmony. Play both allows and requires us to do that, to seek that synchronization.

That, I think, is why so many people play golf and why golf is the greatest game in the world. It is an endless challenge. And it is play.

You will search long and in vain, I suspect, for an endeavor that combines the challenges and pleasures of golf. It tests your body, not for brute strength but for strength tempered by coordination and grace. It tests your mind for the ability to learn, to strategize, to remain calm under pressure. It tests you for qualities of character that I greatly admire: persistence, patience, and determination. Golf challenges you to measure yourself against a universally recognized standard of excellence, par. More than that, it challenges you to better not just an opponent, but yourself.

It is the most honest sport I know. You can't fake golf skills. You can't hide behind the skills of teammates. At the end of a round, you can't tell yourself you played well if you haven't.

It is a sport you can never master, never cease to learn. It will never bore you. And boredom, I suspect, is at the root of many of the plagues of modern life.

I think this is why people invented golf. It gives us the playful pleasures of being outdoors in good company, of striking a ball and making it fly a long way—and it challenges us. It satisfies our need to face difficulties and surmount them. Golf makes our lives fuller and more complete—if we maintain the balance between challenge and play.

When I talk to people about the challenge of becoming good at golf, I sometimes promise that if they commit themselves to a process of improvement, they will have a ball finding out how good they can get. One listener recently objected.

"Wait a minute, Doc," he said. "If I practice and take lessons for weeks and weeks and then don't improve when I play, I'm not having a ball. I'm discouraged, disappointed, and unhappy."

True enough. People can and do err in the direction of getting too serious about their golf. I sometimes talk with retirees who tell me how much they looked forward to be-

ing able to spend all day, every day, working at their golf.
But after a few months, they say, the game doesn't seem like
fun any more.

The reason, I suspect, was their approach to the game.
They wanted to work at it. They transferred to golf the attitudes they had had toward their jobs, and changed it from
a game to a job, from play to drudgery. They expected that
their handicaps would drop in response to their efforts with
the same regularity that their paychecks rose on the job.
When that didn't happen, they stopped having fun at golf. It
was their attitudes that defeated them, not the nature of the
game or the challenge of improvement.

So, as you progress through this program toward the golf
of your dreams, remember that it's not a job. If you are going to honor the commitment you've made, there probably
will be times when you have to prod yourself to do your
putting drills or your stretching exercises, but you can't let
them become drudgery. Remember that golf is something
you chose to play. It's something you've admitted to yourself you would like to play better. You're practicing not
because you want to work harder than anyone else, but because you know practice will eventually make you better,
and you want to savor the joy of playing the best golf you
can play. You practice your putting because you know that
someday, that practice will allow you to walk onto a green
and think, *it's party time.* You practice because practice will
eventually make the game easier and effortless. The more
you understand golf, the simpler and more instinctive the

game will seem to you. The better you play, the less fatigue you'll feel at the end of a round.

When I say you'll have a ball finding out how good you can get, I don't mean that the process will be all smiles and giggles. I mean that you'll experience many of the emotions that life offers, including frustration, disappointment, and despair. I mean that you'll be able to take pride in having the mental tenacity to persevere in the face of those emotions. And I mean that when, having persevered, you finally do your best, when you put things together and play well, you will feel twice as happy about it, twice as proud of what you have accomplished, because of the travail you faced along the way.

If it were easy, you wouldn't experience this joy, any more than you experience joy when you satisfy your hunger by picking up the phone and ordering pizza.

Some people who take up the challenge of golf later object that the game isn't fair. To which I reply, "You're right. Golf is not fair."

It isn't fair that Tiger Woods and Laura Davies got so much more talent than most of us. It isn't fair that some people got expert tutelage early in life and never developed bad swings to overcome. It isn't fair that one player's mishit ball will strike a tree, carom onto the green, and roll up next to the pin while another's will strike the same tree, carom deeper into the woods, and be lost.

So what? Would you like life to be perfectly fair? Would you like to pay the full price for all the mistakes you've gotten away with? Would you like to give back all the advantages you've been given? The fact is that golf, like life, deals us all a set of circumstances, and our challenge is to make the best of them. If you love golf, if you love life, then you love its caprices.

As my friend Tom Kite says, if you love golf, you love it when you've got it in the palm of your hand, and you love it when you can't find it. You love it when you win on Sunday, and you love it when you fall on your face. You love it when it breaks your heart.

And it will, at times, break your heart. You may work on your short game, go to the course, chip and putt beautifully—and shoot the same old score because your long swing has gotten away from you and you can't stop hitting your tee shots into the woods. Or you may put everything else together and find that you can't putt.

That's when you will have to find the strength within yourself to stay the course. That's when you have to keep your dream in the front of your mind. That's when you have to arm yourself with reasons to continue.

That's when you have to say to yourself, *I love golf. I really admire people who get good at it. It's a hard game and it takes time. But I will really feel good about myself when I get there.*

If you can find the strength to think this way, to be patient and persistent and yet always playful, there will be a glorious payoff. It may take longer than you expect or want, but, at some point, things will start to fall into place. The three-foot putts will start falling consistently, rolling firmly into the middle of the cup. The chips and little pitches will start to spring off your club face with crisp, controlled authority. You'll love to watch them roll and curl to a stop by the hole.

Maybe it will be a sudden moment of grace and clarity, a feeling of *ah, so that's it*. Or it might happen gradually and quietly, so that it won't be noticed until you're taking a long walk to a green with a putter in your hand and you realize how many of your irons have been flying straight to the flag.

In a game that is rich with sweet moments, these will be the sweetest of all. These will be among the sweetest moments of your life.

# APPENDIX A

## ROTELLA'S RULES

- The good news about golf is that great physical ability is not required to play well.

- Characteristics like desire, patience, and persistence, more than physical talent, are what enable athletes in any sport to improve their performance.

- If you're going to get better at golf or at anything else that requires disciplined effort, you must first think of yourself as capable of becoming a fine golfer. You must believe that you have the talent to succeed.

- What's most important about a pro is not what he charges. It's the joy he takes in helping golfers develop. It's his dedication to the game and his profession. It's what he knows, and his skill in communicating it.

- If the pupil isn't learning, the teacher isn't teaching.

- No one is too old to learn.

- At some point, any golfer who wants to get better must make a commitment to a teacher, and he must make a commitment to a process of improvement.

- If you want to improve your golf game, you have to accept long periods when your efforts can seem wasted, when your scores don't reflect the effort you're putting in. These will be the times when patience and perseverance will be the most important traits you can have.

- Only practice counts as practice.

- The playing lesson is a great diagnostic tool. It shows the pro what his pupil's game is really like.

- It's on the holes where they don't hit the greens that the scratch player often separates himself from the six-handicapper.

- As you embark on a swing change, it's important to know that two of the chief challenges you face are habit and comfort.

- You need good, sound, dominant habits.

- If you decide that you love striving to get better, you can always make yourself happy by working at your game.

- However you manage it, practicing with a focused mind will make your practice more efficient and beneficial.

- Parents ought to lay down certain rules of behavior for their young golfers. They ought to require that a child meet minimal standards for behavior, temper, sportsmanship, and grades in school if he or she is to continue playing and taking lessons. But they should not try to teach the backswing.

- Self-discipline is not a quality, like blue eyes, that people either have or don't have at birth. Every time they face a situation requiring discipline, people either talk themselves into sticking with a plan or they talk themselves out of it.

- Real talent is patience. It's persistence. It's the ability always to keep in mind the vision of yourself as you want to be.

# YOUR IMPROVEMENT
# PROGRAM

Take notes on each lesson and practice session. They'll help you remember what you've learned and chart your progress. Copy these pages and use them each time you go through an improvement cycle.

LESSON ONE _____

_____

_____

_____

PRACTICE SESSION I _____

_____

_____

PRACTICE II _____

_____

PRACTICE III _____

_____

PRACTICE IV _____

_____

PRACTICE V _____

_____

PLAY (COURSE AND SCORE)_____

PLAY (COURSE AND SCORE)_____

PRACTICE VI _____

_____

PRACTICE VII _____

_____

PRACTICE VIII _____

_____

PRACTICE IX _____

_____

PLAY (COURSE AND SCORE)_____

PLAY (COURSE AND SCORE)_____

LESSON TWO _____
_____
_____
_____

PRACTICE X _____
_____

PRACTICE XI _____
_____

PRACTICE XII _____

PRACTICE XIII _____
_____

PLAY (COURSE AND SCORE)_____

PLAY (COURSE AND SCORE)_____

PRACTICE XIV _____
_____

PRACTICE XV_____
_____

PRACTICE XVI _____

_____

PRACTICE XVII _____

_____

PRACTICE XVIII _____

_____

PLAY (COURSE AND SCORE) _____

PLAY (COURSE AND SCORE) _____

LESSON THREE _____

_____

_____

_____

PRACTICE XIX _____

_____

PRACTICE XX _____

_____

PRACTICE XXI _____

_____

PRACTICE XXII _____

_____

PLAY (COURSE AND SCORE)_____

PLAY (COURSE AND SCORE)_____

PRACTICE XXIII _____

_____

PRACTICE XXIV _____

_____

PRACTICE XXV _____

_____

PRACTICE XXVI _____

_____

PRACTICE XXVII _____

_____

PLAY (COURSE AND SCORE)_____

PLAY (COURSE AND SCORE)_____

LESSON FOUR _____

_____

_____

_____


PRACTICE XXVIII _____

_____


PRACTICE XXIX _____

_____


PRACTICE XXX _____

_____


PRACTICE XXXI _____

_____


PLAY (COURSE AND SCORE) _____


PLAY (COURSE AND SCORE) _____


LESSON FIVE _____

_____

_____

_____


PRACTICE XXXII _____

_____

PRACTICE XXXIII _____

_____

PRACTICE XXXIV _____

_____

PRACTICE XXXV _____

_____

PLAY (CHARTED ROUND) _____

    No. 1. SHOTS: _____ TOTAL: _____

    No. 2. SHOTS: _____ TOTAL: _____

    No. 3. SHOTS: _____ TOTAL: _____

    No. 4. SHOTS: _____ TOTAL: _____

    No. 5. SHOTS: _____ TOTAL: _____

    No. 6. SHOTS: _____ TOTAL: _____

    No. 7. SHOTS: _____ TOTAL: _____

    No. 8. SHOTS: _____ TOTAL: _____

    No. 9. SHOTS: _____ TOTAL: _____

    No. 10. SHOTS: _____ TOTAL: _____

    No. 11. SHOTS: _____ TOTAL: _____

    No. 12. SHOTS: _____ TOTAL: _____

NO. 13. SHOTS: _____ TOTAL: _____

NO. 14: SHOTS: _____ TOTAL: _____

NO. 15: SHOTS: _____ TOTAL: _____

NO. 16: SHOTS: _____ TOTAL: _____

NO. 17: SHOTS: _____ TOTAL: _____

NO. 18: SHOTS: _____ TOTAL: _____

TOTAL SHOTS: _____
SHOTS FROM WITHIN 120 YARDS OF
THE HOLE: _____

PERCENTAGE OF TEE SHOTS IN
PLAY: _____

PERCENTAGE OF PUTTS UNDER FIVE
FEET MADE: _____

PERCENTAGE OF UP-AND-DOWN
CHANCES CONVERTED: _____

PERCENTAGE OF SAND SAVES: _____

PLAY (CHARTED ROUND) _____

NO. 1. SHOTS: _____ TOTAL: _____

NO. 2. SHOTS: _____ TOTAL: _____

NO. 3. SHOTS: _____ TOTAL: _____

No.  4.  Shots: _____ Total: _____

No.  5.  Shots: _____ Total: _____

No.  6.  Shots: _____ Total: _____

No.  7.  Shots: _____ Total: _____

No.  8.  Shots: _____ Total: _____

No.  9.  Shots: _____ Total: _____

No. 10.  Shots: _____ Total: _____

No. 11.  Shots: _____ Total: _____

No. 12.  Shots: _____ Total: _____

No. 13.  Shots: _____ Total: _____

No. 14:  Shots: _____ Total: _____

No. 15:  Shots: _____ Total: _____

No. 16:  Shots: _____ Total: _____

No. 17:  Shots: _____ Total: _____

No. 18:  Shots: _____ Total: _____

Total shots:_____ Shots from
within 120 yards of the hole:_____

Percentage of tee shots in
play:_____

PERCENTAGE OF PUTTS UNDER FIVE
FEET MADE:_____

PERCENTAGE OF UP-AND-DOWN
CHANCES CONVERTED:_____

PERCENTAGE OF SAND SAVES:_____

PRACTICE XXXVI_____
_____

PRACTICE XXXVII_____
_____

PRACTICE XXXVIII_____
_____

PRACTICE XXXIX_____
_____

PRACTICE XL_____
_____

LESSON SIX (PLAYING LESSON)_____
_____
_____
_____

FIVE DAYS OFF

# A C K N O W L E D G E M E N T S

The list of people who helped with this book is a long one. It begins with all coaches I have known over the years in many sports. By watching them and listening to them, I have learned much about the dedication, faith, and commitment involved in preparing an athlete for peak performance. I've seen the joy that the best coaches derive from helping human beings honor a commitment, focus their minds, and attain their dreams. I've learned that coaching is truly a noble profession.

I must thank as well the athletes who have honored me with their confidence over the years. They've shown me how to chase a dream doing something they love.

More specifically, I am indebted to the golfers—professional and amateur—whom I've worked with. I suspect I learned as much from each of them as they learned from me about the way people get better at golf. I owe much as well to the teaching pros I have been privileged to call colleagues over the years—at *Golf Digest* schools, at the National Golf Foundation, in the PGA of America.

Then there are the individuals whose names you've read in the pages of this book—Rob McNamara and Gene Hilen; Hank Johnson; David and Greg Belcher; Paul Buckley and Pete Mathews; Alice Hovde and Todd Anderson; Bill Davis, Patty Pilz, and Jay and Arline Hoffman; Bob Toski; Kandi Kessler-Comer and Phil Owenby; Dan Grider and Terry Crouch; Dan and Michael Henderson; Mark Heartfield and Dick Kreitler; Robert Willis and Mike Carver; and Rocco Mediate. Each of them gave generously of time, insight, and, in many cases, hospitality. More than that, they gave inspiration. I am thankful to them all.

I've also benefitted from the advice of a number of people who commented on this project while it was in progress, including Bill Heron, Rod Thompson, and my parents, Laura and Guy Rotella.

I am grateful as well to my agent, Wally Buchleitner, and to my editor at Simon & Schuster, Dominick Anfuso, who is a genius at titles, concepts, dust jackets, and general guidance.

Finally, thanks to Casey and Darlene Rotella for their kindness and patience with the disruptions this project caused.